VAGABOND READERS

A CONTRACT READING PROGRAM FOR GRADES 4-9

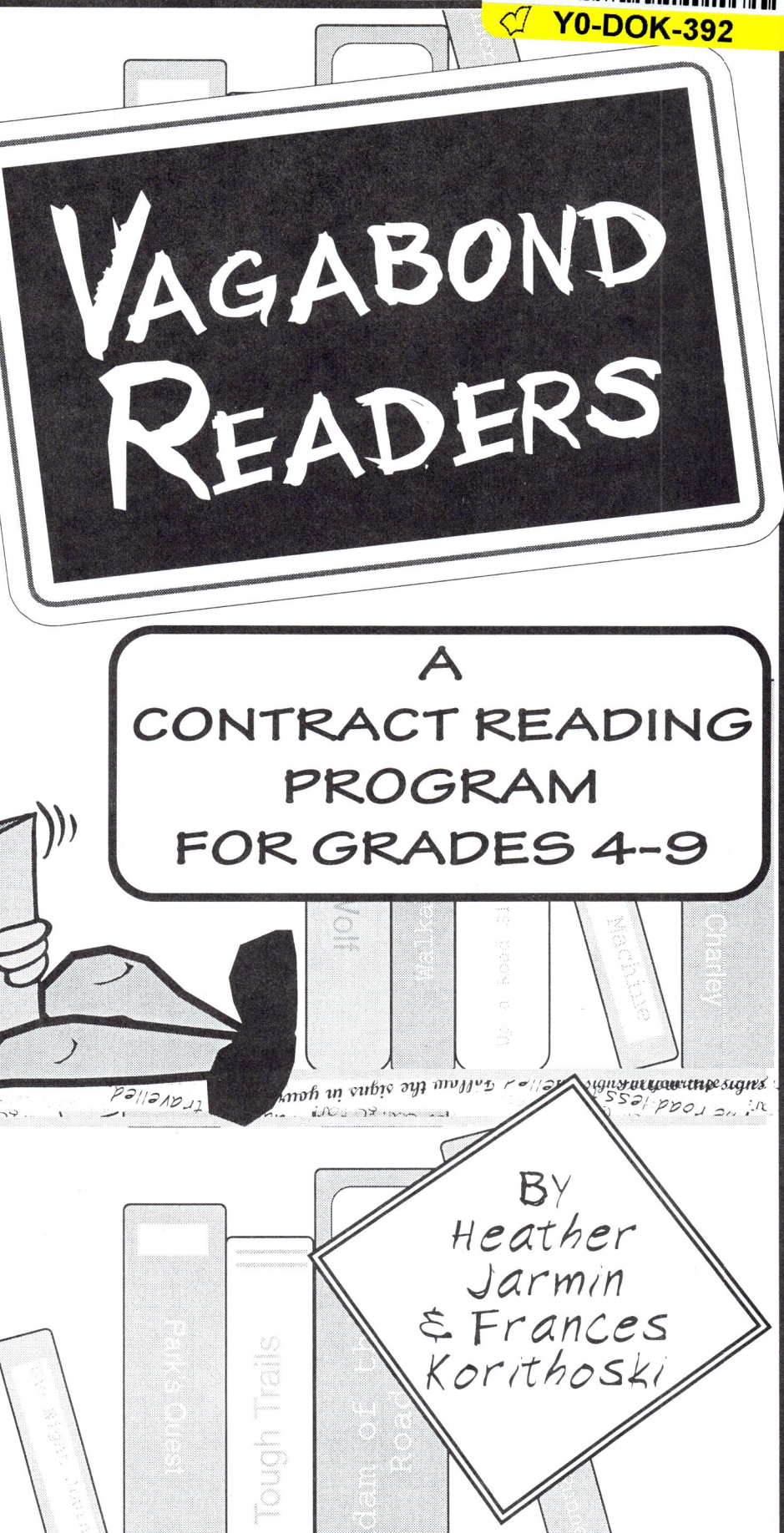

BY
Heather
Jarmin
& Frances
Korithoski

Vagabond Readers: A Contract Reading Program
by Heather Jarmin and Frances Korithoski
ISBN: 0-9699619-3-6

F. P. Hendriks Publishing Ltd.

Main Office   **US Office**
4806–53 St.   1214 Flint Hill Road
Stettler, Alberta, Canada T0C 2L2   Wilmington, DE, USA 19808-1914

Phone/Fax: 403-742-6483
Toll Free Phone/Fax: 1-888-374-8787
E-mail: hendriks@telusplanet.net
Website: www.telusplanet.net/public/hendriks

Canadian Cataloguing in Publication Data
Jarmin, Heather, 1966-
  Vagabond readers

  Includes bibliographic references.
  ISBN 0-9699619-3-6

  1. Reading (Elementary)—Activity programs. 2. Reading
(Secondary)—Activity programs. 3. School libraries—Activity programs.
4. Children—Books and reading. I. Korithoski, Frances, 1950- II. Title.
LB1050.J37 1997   372.42'7   C97-9109677-X

Production Team
Thanks to all those talented people who worked on this project:

Authors	Heather Jarmin, Frances Korithoski
Cartoons	Carl Horak (Custom Cartoons)
Project Director	Faye Boer
Editors	Faye Boer, Barbara Demers
Page Layout and Design	Christine Jilek (Heartland Promotions)
Cover Design	Christine Jilek (Heartland Promotions)
Photography	Philip Jarmin
Production Assistant	Joni Campbell

Manufacturer
Print Stop Inc.
Stettler Independent (cover)
PRINTED IN CANADA
2nd printing

TABLE OF CONTENTS

Charting New Territory

Heather: Kori, this year I'd like to handle my library class differently. I don't feel that it is meeting my goals for my students or their needs. Some students seem to spend all their time looking for books and I have no way of directing their reading or even knowing if they are reading at all. Do you have any ideas?

Kori: We could turn the free reading time in your language arts class into a structured reading time in the library.

Heather: That doesn't sound like much fun. We have a library period so students can choose the books they enjoy.

Heather, teacher

Kori: Think of it this way. You wouldn't go on a trip without planning and making arrangements first. The structure can be like travel plans as students "book" various journeys in literature. We can include activities that will hold their interest. It could be a lot of fun!

Heather: This is starting to sound great but it could mean a lot of extra work. The program has to be manageable for me.

Kori: It may save you time in the long run because we can easily tie it into your language arts program. For example, some library classes might be used for speaking activities.

Heather: I could also incorporate writing skills and vocabulary.

Kori: We could have the students link each reading achievement to a short written assignment to be shared with the entire class.

Kori, librarian

Heather: It would certainly be easy to relate their reading experiences to literature concepts that we study during the year in our regular Language Arts classes.

Kori: We could let them decide on the grade they wish to achieve and how they wish to achieve their goals. This could help them take responsibility for their own learning.

Heather: This is also an opportunity to involve the parents in the goal-setting process.

Kori: The new format will bring structure and substance to the reading program. Students will learn that library class is a real part of their learning requiring ongoing effort to achieve goals they have set for themselves. They'll also realize as they approach their goals, that the best part of the trip is not necessarily the arriving but it is the journey!

Vagabond Readers
© 1997 F.P. Hendriks Publishing Ltd.

These Boots Were Made for Walking—Background

Story-writing is no longer an educational fad. It has become the main emphasis in teaching language skills to students in the elementary grades and continuing into junior high. For teachers, the struggle is in how to teach story-writing most effectively. What works? What doesn't? By asking questions and examining various teaching methods we came upon a simple, yet often overlooked relationship—*to write well, it is necessary to read good literature.*

How do children learn to speak years before entering a classroom? Infants learn by mimicking the sounds they hear around them. As they grow older, infants string these sounds together copying the examples they hear. By age three or four, infants' speech reflects the language of significant people in their lives—parents, siblings, babysitters, and other relatives. Generally speaking, if an infant's speech models use language correctly, then the infant will learn to speak correctly as well.

The question is—What does learning to speak correctly have to do with teaching writing? Just as children become effective speakers by imitating good models of spoken language, so do they become effective writers by imitating good models of written language. Exposure to good written models requires that the children read or listen to good literature.

For the purposes of this book, **good literature** is defined as *books and stories that provide varied and complex reading experiences and demonstrate specific writing techniques, such as characterization, foreshadowing, and so on.* The more exposure children have to such models of writing, the more proficient their writing will become.

FINDING BOOTS THAT FIT

Because they believe that a relationship exists between reading good books and writing well, language arts teachers faithfully bring classes to the library or learning resource center one or more times per week, hoping that the improvement in students' writing will occur naturally. However, once inside the library door, many students head directly for the first garishly-illustrated cover that catches their attention. Others wander aimlessly or browse through new materials that are generously illustrated. Still others sit quietly with glazed eyes fastened on a page that never seems to turn.

How then do teachers expose students to examples of good literature on a regular basis? Visits by published authors lack regularity and when reading times are labeled "free," it is difficult to ensure that good literature is being read or that students are reading at all.

When we first became involved in teaching Grade 7 Language Arts, we were shocked to learn that many students regularly signed books out from the school library but did not actually finished reading them. An organized reading program conducted, such as *Vagabond Readers*, on its own or in conjunction with a language arts program can help to solve this dilemma.

STEPPING OUT

Contracted reading means that students, along with their teachers and parents, decide on reading goals and establish schedules for achieving those goals. As students read more regularly and are exposed to models of good writing, they will begin to use techniques that published authors use in their writing. Reading good literature allows students to develop more diverse vocabularies and a broader general knowledge. Because their imaginations are stimulated, they look forward to sharing their reading experiences with their classmates. These results come about both directly and indirectly when students are encouraged to open a book and actually read.

THE ROAD WE ARE TAKING

The reading program described in this book makes use of student contracts referred to as "passports" and focuses on the connection between reading and writing. It also links students' experiences with literature to other aspects of the language curriculum such as listening, speaking, viewing, and creating.

The specific learner expectations of the program are as follows:

1. Students are motivated to set monthly reading goals and follow schedules to achieve their goals.
2. Students help achieve a climate conducive to enjoyable reading experiences.
3. Students develop an interest in a variety of literary genre.
4. Students use reading as a foundation for building other language skills, particularly writing.

These expectations will be achieved by

1. contracting monthly reading goals that correspond to a percentage grade or letter grade,
2. enlisting the support of parents to help their children set monthly reading goals and to develop and maintain schedules for reaching those goals,
3. incorporating various activities and projects to link reading to learner expectations in the language arts curriculum,
4. including high-interest activities for students to share aspects of their reading with others, and
5. including students' levels of reading achievement in their term progress reports.

The program delivered in *Vagabond Readers* is intended to help you and your students start off on the right foot for the trek to your own unique destinations in literature. We wish you luck on your journeys into the fascinating and exciting realm of literature.

Happy Reading,
Heather and Kori

Preparing for the Trip—Advance Planning

TEACHER:

- decides, with students, on format for log books: e.g., index cards in folders, cards attached to card-holders, photocopied pages in duotangs.
- prepares materials for log books: e.g., folders or card-holders, and pre-formatted log entries.
- photocopies record-keeping forms for own use.
- prepares student passports (contracts).
- prepares survey handouts and letters for parents.
- may divide class into teams for the purpose of tracking reading progress on classroom charts or maps.
- may select destinations to correspond with monthly reading goals. These may include locales the students are studying in other curricular areas (see Sack of Suggestions, page 14).

STUDENTS:

- may be asked to complete reading surveys at home prior to the first class.
- may help in making a class map or chart for tracking individual or team progress towards reading destinations or goals. If preferred, an enlarged version of the teacher's Record of Log Entries may be mounted on poster board and laminated for this purpose. (See the section on Record-keeping in the Appendix, pages 147–161.)
- may decorate their folders or card-holders before the first class.
- may choose a name for their class team and design or select appropriate stickers or stamps for tracking progress on the classroom chart or map.

Hitting the Hot Spots—Activities

TEACHER:

- provides instruction on skills related to reading, writing, and the use of the library.
- provides direction for activities.

STUDENTS:

- complete exercises.
- participate in activities.
- carry out assignments individually, unless otherwise directed.
- provide neatly-written products demonstrating attention to writing conventions.

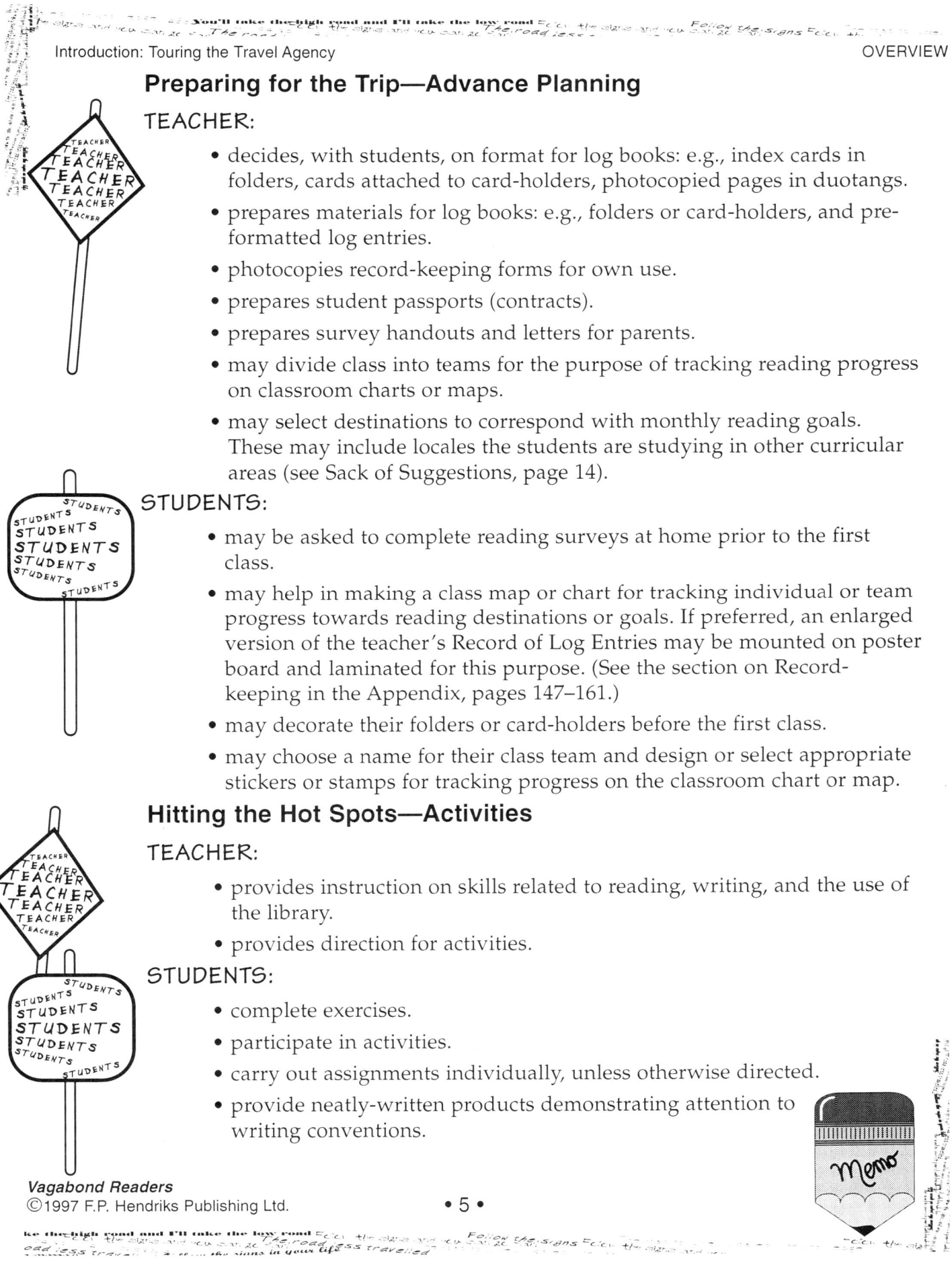

Completing Log Book Entries—Formatted Cards

TEACHER:

- provides instruction on the completion of various types of pre-formatted log book entry cards, each of which may include:

    1. a bibliography or biblio-bridge;
    2. the classification of the novel;
    3. the required number of informative points about the story:

        a) 7 points in complete sentences

           or

        b) 14 points in note form. (See lessons on completing log entries in Chapter Two.)

- ensures that students understand the correlation between number of books successfully logged and letter grades.

STUDENTS:

- read novels.
- choose a format and complete a log entry for each novel read.
- provide a neatly-written product demonstrating attention to writing conventions.
- correct errors on each log entry as required until the entry meets an acceptable standard.

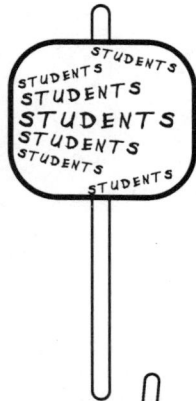

Celebrating!—Enrichment

TEACHER:

- discusses possible projects.
- explains his or her expectations of the student.

STUDENTS:

- select a project.
- complete project by due date according to teacher's expectations.

Keeping Track—Assessment and Record-keeping

TEACHER:

- uses assessment form to grade log entries, returning for corrections those not meeting the required standard.
- records corrected log entries as submitted by students.
- records participation in activities.
- records satisfactory completion of Student Performance Masters and celebration projects.

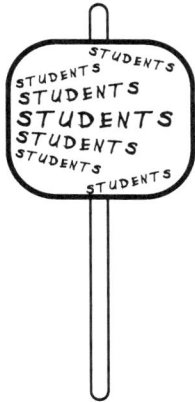

STUDENTS:

- insert completed entries into log books where they may be retrieved by the teacher for assessment.
- place a marker in the appropriate place on classroom or personal record for each log entry approved by the teacher. (See the Record-keeping section in the Appendix, pages 147–161.)

Teaching and Learning Tools Found in the Book

GUIDED GLOBETROTTING—Overview of Lessons in Chapters One to Five

The lessons in this book begin in Chapter One.

Chapter One includes

- suggestions for orienting your students to the library
- student evaluations of personal reading habits
- metacognition activities related to choosing reading material
- suggestions for launching the program in your classroom
- sample reading surveys
- sample letters to parents

Chapter Two includes

- specific lessons on using the library
- instruction on writing bibliographies
- lessons on completing log entries
- ideas for relating reading to students' writing

Chapter Three includes

- genres of literature and how to distinguish them

Chapter Four includes

- activities to direct the students toward discovering the link between their own writing and the concepts taught in writing lessons

Chapter Five includes

- suggestions for enriching oral and written activities for the sharing of reading experiences
- ideas for celebrating the students' reading

Many of the lessons include whole-class activities. Resources called for in the lessons such as blackline masters of Overhead Projections are provided directly following the corresponding lesson. These Overhead Projections may also be reproduced as student handouts or as classroom charts. This book has been organized with lessons followed by Overhead Projections, Student Performance Masters, Student References, and Teacher References.

TROUBLESHOOTING—Travel Insurance

Found at the end of this Introduction, Travel Insurance is designed to help the classroom teacher deal with problems that may arise in carrying out the program. It covers such topics as coping with time constraints, renegotiating student contracts, and modifying lesson plans for integrated special needs students. References on wax seal and ribbon icons direct the teacher to the Travel Insurance pages.

IDEAS PLUS—Sack of Suggestions

Included here are ideas for motivating and encouraging students, as well as a suggestion for integrating the program with the Social Studies curriculum. A reference to this section, if included, will be at the end of the chapter.

DESTINATIONS—Correlation of Grades with Reading Goals

Chapter One includes Overhead Projection Masters that provide correlations between the number of books read with letter grades and/or the destinations named on record-keeping maps. These correlations are provided only as guidelines. The individual teacher or librarian is encouraged to adapt his or her program to suit the students. An Overhead Projection that allows the teacher to write in adapted goals is provided.

VAGABOND READER PASSPORT—The Reading Contract

The introductory lesson in Chapter One presents the reading contract to students, and provides preliminary instruction in goal-setting. The contract is signed by the student, her parent(s), and the teacher. It specifies the student's intended goal and destination, and becomes her "passport" to literary adventures. The teacher agrees to assign the mark that corresponds to the destination reached (goal achieved) by the student. The parent's commitment is to support and encourage the child in her reading at home. Reading contracts may be adjusted if the student finds that her chosen goal is unrealistic (see Travel Insurance, page 10).

VAGABOND LOG BOOK AND LOG ENTRIES—Card-holder and Cards

The student "logs" his reading experiences by filling out index cards or photocopied sheets in a variety of formats. Completed entries are then filed in the student log book, which may take the form of a folder, duotang, or card-holder. The log books should be stored where they can be accessed easily by the teacher for marking or by other interested students. Like a real traveler's log, the student's collection of cards provides an anchor or frame of reference for thoughts and feelings associated with his reading travels. Suggested formats, found in Chapter Two, include a summary paragraph, a story gift shop, a diary entry, a plot time line, a newspaper article, and others.

SIGNPOSTS & ALTERNATE ROUTE SIGNS—Information for the Teacher

These messages provide information that the teacher may find especially helpful in implementing individual lessons and activities.

TOOLS FOR TRAVELING—Assessment and Record-Keeping Forms

The Appendix contains a tested assessment checklist for grading log entries, answer sheets for Overhead Projections and Student Performance Masters, and record-keeping forms that may be used for reporting purposes. If desired, these may be used just as they appear. The teacher or librarian may also adapt them to suit his or her needs as well as the needs of the students.

Travel Insurance

What if . . .

- **students are not honest in their answers to the reading survey?** (Chapter One)

Despite the assurance that their answers cannot be right or wrong, some students may still answer the survey questions with what they think their parents or teachers want to hear. This can be avoided by having the students fill out their surveys at home with their parents or by having the students share their answers with one another in small groups. This form of sharing usually encourages the students to answer honestly for fear their dishonest answers will be recognized by either parent or peer. Another approach to this problem may be to ensure that the students are able to complete the survey in private and that their answers will remain confidential. If neither approach is possible, then wait until later in the program when it becomes evident that there are inconsistencies between the students' answers and their behaviors. Then sit down with individual students privately and discuss their surveys together. Avoid making the students feel as if they have done something wrong. Rather, approach this as a re-evaluation after the program has begun. It might be useful to re-evaluate all students so that some do not feel singled out.

- **students do not return their contracts?** (Chapter One)

There is always the risk when sending something home with students that it may never return. Set a due date for the return of the contracts. If after this date a student still has not returned a contract, then arrange for a private conference with that student at recess, lunch hour, or during reading period while the other students are involved in their own work. Discuss the survey and goals with the student and together sign a realistic contract for him or her.

- **students are not realistic about the number of books they are able to read?** (Chapter One)

On occasion students will, despite all efforts by teacher or parents, choose goals that do not match their abilities. Wait. If they insist on setting these goals, then at least let them try to achieve them. You may be surprised. Decide on a trial period. If a student appears to be struggling and it seems unlikely that he or she will reach reach an intended goal, schedule a time when you can review the student's progress in private. Renegotiate another contract that will satisfy the student while allowing him or her to experience some success. You may also do this at set times throughout the year with the entire class. It allows students to opt out of unrealistic contracts and reminds them, at the same time, of the goals they have set.

Travel Insurance, continued

Travel
Insurance

What if...

- **the reading scales on the "Destinations" Overhead Projection Masters correlating grades and reading goals are not appropriate for my students?** (Chapter One)

The reading scales supplied on the "Destinations" Overhead Projection Masters were arrived at following an informal survey of students and teachers to determine average reading habits and capabilities at each grade level. These scales reflect such factors as the shorter length of books (usually under 100 pages) read by upper elementary students in comparison to those read at the middle school level (usually around 150 pages) and in Grade 9 (often 200 pages and up). The teacher is encouraged to adapt scales as necessary in order to challenge and/or motivate both proficient and reluctant readers in his or her own individual classroom.

- **our school does not have an interested teacher or an interested librarian with whom I can work?** (Chapter Two)

This program works well when a classroom teacher and a librarian work together and communicate with each other about the areas of need for the students, lessons, and activities. However, **a partnership is not necessary**. The *Vagabond Readers* program will also work well for one teacher or one librarian who wishes to implement it.

- **students prefer lower quality "series" or "pulp" fiction?** (Chapter Three)

Students of upper elementary and junior high school age are often drawn to series fiction that has high emotional appeal but questionable literary merit. Such books may serve a valuable purpose, however, because

a) they often initiate youngsters into a phase of voracious, emotion-driven reading during which their competence increases dramatically.

b) due to the high-interest factor, it is often via series or pulp fiction that children first "lose" themselves in their reading.

Reading of this type should not be completely discouraged. However, we suggest that students be limited to a maximum of three to five books from a particular series or by a particular author so that these students may be exposed to a variety of genres.

- **I teach the lessons but students continue to have trouble with the activities required?** (Chapter Three)

This program's content covers a wide range of material, so students will probably have to be reminded of concepts previously taught. Review often. Go back in the book and choose activities you did not do initially or repeat others in order to reinforce the concepts with your students.

Travel Insurance, continued

What if...

• I don't have time to grade log entries? (Chapter Three)

Evaluate log entries with students during the library classes while students are reading or working on other log book entries. Discuss areas where improvement is needed and also mention areas of strength. Students tend to thrive on one-to-one attention; you will be targeting their areas of need and you won't be spending time out of class marking. Also, when you take time out during the reading period to talk to students about their work, it breaks up the reading time and helps some students stay on task.

• some of my students choose the same format for each log entry they complete? (Chapter Three)

You may want to limit the number of log entries that you will accept from a student in any one format, especially if capable students are continually choosing the simpler formats. Discretion is needed, however. Students with learning disabilities and/or special needs may require formats that allow them to present information in note form. These students should not be penalized for using the same format several times, provided they are putting their best effort into their work.

• I can't work in all the activities in the program? (Chapter Four)

As more and more demands are put on schools and the classroom teacher each year, the common response to new materials and programs is "I don't have time for that." That is why *Vagabond Readers* is designed to fit in with existing curriculum constraints in order to enrich a program rather than replace it. Remember the conversation the two teachers had at the beginning of the book? Through this program you may deal with many concepts from the curriculum and at the same time encourage your students to become more enthusiastic readers. Further, the program is flexible. The focus is on reading and its relationship to writing.

First select those activities that suit your program and that interest you the most. Other lessons can be reviewed later in the year as time allows. In some cases the program can be continued and even extended the following year. Keep in mind that reading is the most basic of curriculum requirements. If we can instill in students a desire to read for enjoyment, then it makes the achievement of all other curriculum goals that much easier.

Travel Insurance, continued

Travel
Insurance

What about . . .

- **integrated Special Needs students?**

It is important to find reading materials that accommodate both the interests and the skills of special needs students. The librarian will be able to assist in locating age-appropriate books that are written at the required vocabulary level. With the help of parents and/or the special needs teacher, help the student decide on a goal that challenges but does not overwhelm him or her. Limit the requirements for written assignments and other activities to what you feel the individual student is able to handle. In some cases, adaptations may be necessary. Other students who master the concepts easily may be happy to provide assistance by "buddying up" with those having special needs.

- **incorporating grades for reporting purposes?**

The grade for each student can be factored in with those for each term or it can be factored into a final grade only. If anecdotal grading is used, then a statement of the student's achievement in comparison to his or her goal is sufficient to communicate progress to the student and to the parent. If the parents have been involved in determining the contract, then they will understand whether their child is working to her potential or whether she needs to put more effort into reading.

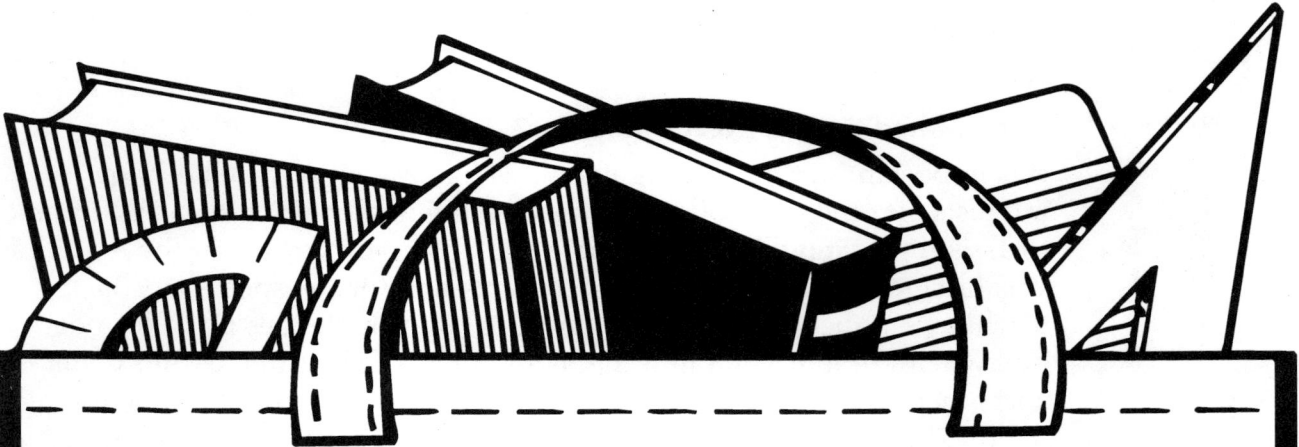

Sack of Suggestions

- The *Vagabond Readers* program can be linked successfully with other subjects, particularly at the upper elementary and middle school levels. One suggestion, mentioned in the Overview as well, is to relate monthly reading goals to destinations (places on the globe) the students are studying in other classes. In this way the Social Studies or Science program may be integrated into Language Arts. Maps of the areas may be enlarged and made available to the students. Each book or group of books read by a student may represent a certain unit of distance on the map. Thus, the more the student reads, the more areas he is able to explore. This visual record of reading often motivates those students who are not enticed by grades alone.

  E.g., For certain curricula, Grades four and five may use a map of China to record their progress, the farthest distances being equal to the highest grades achieved. A grade six class may use a map of Ancient Greece, grade seven students could use Japan, and so on.

- If it is not possible or feasible for a classroom teacher to integrate other subjects, destinations on a map, globe, or in space can still be used as visual records and student motivators. The teacher may choose random destinations to correlate with the number of books read, or the students may be asked to vote on or suggest their own list of destinations. The farthest distance is always equal to the highest grade achievable.

Getting Itchy Feet!

Heather: My students are eager to start their adventures in literature. They've even come up with a name for themselves— **Vagabond Readers**.

Kori: Wow! The vagabond image is appealing but it seems a little at odds with our vision of a structured reading program.

Heather: I thought so too at first. On the other hand, the students will choose their own reading goals and progress at their own pace. So within the framework that we give them, they still have choices… perhaps more than they had in their original "free reading" class.

Kori: True. The freedom of the true vagabond may be something or some place that our students find as they journey along their chosen paths.

Heather: So what are we waiting for? Let's start packing!

Meeting with the Travel Agent—Library Orientation

Before allowing students the opportunity to sign out library books, it is necessary to ensure that students know how to look up materials in the catalog and find them on the shelves. An orientation conducted by the librarian or "travel agent" provides them with the information they need to make the best possible use of the available services and resources.

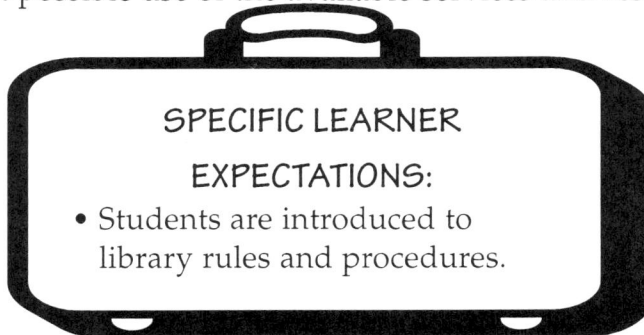

SPECIFIC LEARNER EXPECTATIONS:

- Students are introduced to library rules and procedures.

RESOURCES:

- the library and its signs
- the librarian
- Student Performance Master "Rules of the Road"

TEACHER or LIBRARIAN:

- provides information on:
    - a) library hours
    - b) borrowing period for fiction, nonfiction, reference materials, and audio-visual materials
    - c) library policy regarding noise and behavior
- briefly discusses:
    - a) use of card or computerized catalog
    - b) how to look up books by title, author, and subject
    - c) circulation procedures: how to use the bar code reader; what information is required for signing book cards; where to find the due date
    - d) procedures for handling overdues: where and when overdue notices are posted; policy regarding levying and collection of fines.

STUDENTS:

- complete Student Performance Master "Rules of the Road."

SIGN POST:

To allow adequate time to introduce the program and explain learner expectations, it is best if the logging and recording of reading journeys does not begin until the second month of the school year (usually October). However, encourage students to look for and borrow books at any time after their library orientation so they get an early start on their reading.

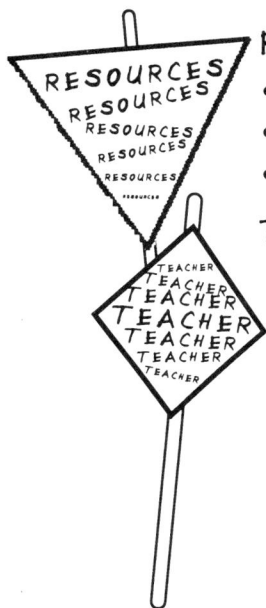

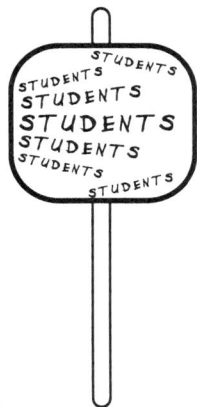

Vagabond Readers
©1997 F.P. Hendriks Publishing Ltd.

STUDENT PERFORMANCE MASTER

NAME _____

RULES OF THE ROAD

1. What are the library's hours?

   _____

2. What is the borrowing period for fiction and nonfiction books?

   _____

3. What kind of cataloging system does your library have—card catalog system or a computerized catalog system?

   _____

4. What information do you use to find a book in the catalog?

   _____

5. Describe the procedure for signing out books.

   _____

   _____

6. What is the policy for borrowing reference items (e.g., encyclopedias)?

   _____

7. What is the policy for borrowing audio-visual materials, such as videos and tapes?

   _____

   _____

8. How do you find out if an item that you have signed out is overdue?

   _____

   _____

9. Does the librarian levy fines for overdue items? If so, how much is the fine?

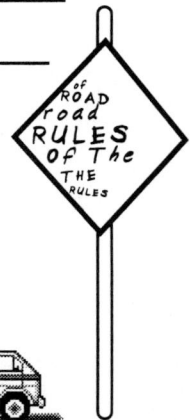

   _____

Studying the Map—An Overview of the Program

Students must have a good understanding of the program before they begin. Just as planning a trip abroad creates anticipation in the traveler, so does active involvement in the program and its components create anticipation in the reader.

SPECIFIC LEARNER EXPECTATIONS:

- The students are introduced to the components of the *Vagabond Readers* program.
- The students (with the help of their parents and the teacher) set realistic monthly reading goals.

RESOURCES:

- age appropriate Student Performance Master "Letter to Parent or Guardian"
- Sample Log Entries (See Chapter Two, pages 66–80)
- Overhead Projection Master "Destinations—Correlation of Grades with Reading Goals" for appropriate grade level
- Student Performance Masters "Thinking About Choices" and/or "Latitude for Attitudes" (to be done in small groups in the class or brought to class already completed with help from parents at home)
- Student Performance Master "Vagabond Reader Passport"

TEACHER:

- prepares examples of essential components of the program to share with the students.
- tells students that the more good literature they read, the better writers they will become.
- explains that the *Vagabond Readers* program is designed to encourage reading through the setting of monthly reading goals.
- explains that the student's chosen goal is a guideline that he or she may or may not reach.
- describes how the goals and destinations relate to grades.
- briefly introduces the various formats for logging reading experiences.
- shows how to complete a passport or contract.
- describes the record-keeping system (chosen in advance; see Advance Planning, page 5 and/or Record-keeping, pages 149–161).

TEACHER AND STUDENTS:

- use the students' reading surveys to discuss setting realistic goals.
- prepare any necessary record-keeping materials (unless this was done in advance).

STUDENTS:

- complete reading surveys in class (unless previously completed at home with parents).
- prepare log books, (unless this was done in advance; see Advance Planning, page 5).
- take the "Letter to Parent" and "Vagabond Reader Passport" home.
- complete the passport with parents' assistance, choosing a realistic monthly reading goal, and return it to the teacher.

SIGN POST:

The yearly goals noted on the "Destinations" Overhead Projection Masters are based on a nine-month period, since it is assumed that logging of reading journeys will not begin until the second month of a typical ten-month year.

The final "Destinations" Overhead Projections Master allows the teacher to write in the number of books necessary to complete reading goals so that the program may be adapted for his or her students' needs.

NAME _____

LETTER TO PARENT OR GUARDIAN OF YOUNGER STUDENT

Date: _____

Dear Parent or Guardian,

As a Grade _____ Language Arts student, your child will be participating in a program entitled *Vagabond Readers*. This program is based on the premise that the more good literature your child reads, the better his or her own story-writing will become. It is designed to encourage reading by relating each book read to a unit of distance traveled.

Your child has been asked to complete the enclosed **Vagabond Reader Passport**, choosing a destination to which he or she will travel by reading. To reach this destination, the student will be required to read a set number of books per month. Your child is encouraged to choose a destination that is realistic for him or her, yet allows room for challenge. The destination acts only as a guideline. The grade your child receives in this program will count as part of his or her final Language Arts mark.

The student will be expected to complete a travel log entry for each book read. These entries may take various forms, but will allow me to ensure that your child understands what he or she is reading. Upon successful completion of a log entry, your child will record one unit of distance toward his or her destination. This travel record will allow individual students to monitor their progress toward their destinations and reading goals.

I would appreciate your involvement in your child's journey in the following ways:

1. Discuss and decide upon a realistic destination with your child (see attached sheet showing reading goals and corresponding grades).
2. Sign your child's **Passport** and return it to school by _____.
3. Help your child set up a schedule that will enable him or her to reach the goal.
4. Encourage your child to read at home during leisure time.
5. Observe your child's reading and offer guidance in his or her choice of books.
6. Discuss books with your child.
7. Be a role model for your child by reading books.

If you have any questions or concerns regarding the *Vagabond Readers* program, please contact me at the school. Thank you for your cooperation.

Sincerely,

_____

(Teacher)

LETTER TO PARENT OR GUARDIAN OF OLDER STUDENTS

Date: _____

Dear Parent or Guardian,

As a Grade _____ Language Arts student, your child will be participating in a program called *Vagabond Readers*. This program is based on the premise that the more good literature your child reads, the better his or her own story-writing will become.

Your child has been asked to complete the enclosed **Vagabond Reader Passport**, choosing a monthly reading goal that is realistic, yet allows room for challenge. To reach this goal, the student will be required to read a certain number of books per month. The goal acts only as a guideline. The grade your child receives in this program will count as part of his or her final Language Arts mark.

The student will be expected to complete a log entry for each book read. These entries may take various forms and will allow me to ensure that your child understands what he or she is reading. Upon successful completion of a log entry, your child will record one book on a reading record. This record will allow individual students to monitor their progress toward their reading goals.

I would appreciate your involvement in your child's program in the following ways:

1. Discuss and decide upon a realistic goal for your child (see the attached sheet showing reading goals and corresponding grades).
2. Sign your child's **Passport** and return it to school by _____.
3. Help your child set up a schedule that will enable him or her to reach the goal.
4. Encourage your child to read at home during leisure time.
5. Observe your child's reading and offer guidance in his or her choice of books.
6. Discuss books with your child.
7. Be a role model for your child by reading books.

If you have any questions or concerns regarding the *Vagabond Readers* program, please contact me at the school. Thank you for your cooperation.

Sincerely,

_____

Teacher

Destinations—Correlation of Grades with Reading Goals

GRADE 4

Number of Books	Destination	Grade
4 per month minimum (36+ for year)	_____	A+
3 per month minimum (27–35 for year)	_____	A
2 per month minimum (18–26 for year)	_____	B
1 per month minimum (9–17 for year)	_____	C
1 per 2 months minimum (4–8 for year)	_____	C-
less than 1 per 2 months (1–3 for year)	_____	D

Destinations—Correlation of Grades with Reading Goals

GRADE 5

Number of Books	Destination	Grade
5 per month minimum (45+ for year)	_____	A+
4 per month minimum (36–44 for year)	_____	A
3 per month minimum (27–35 for year)	_____	B
2 per month minimum (18–26 for year)	_____	C
1 per month minimum (9–17 for year)	_____	C-
less than 1 per month (1–8 for year)	_____	D

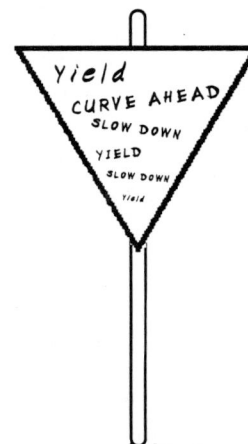

Destinations—Correlation of Grades with Reading Goals

GRADE 6

Number of Books	Destination	Grade
6 per month minimum (54+ for year)	_____	A+
5 per month minimum (45–53 for year)	_____	A
4 per month minimum (36–44 for year)	_____	B
3 per month minimum (27–35 for year)	_____	C
2 per month minimum (18–26 for year)	_____	C-
less than 2 per month (1–17 for year)	_____	D

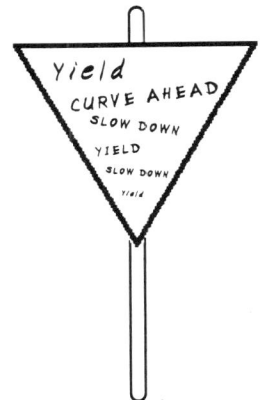

Vagabond Readers
©1997 F.P. Hendriks Publishing Ltd.
Permission to reproduce

Destinations—Correlation of Grades with Reading Goals

GRADE 7

Number of Books	Destination	Grade
4 per month minimum (36+ for year)	_____	A+
3 per month minimum (27–35 for year)	_____	A
2 per month minimum (18–26 for year)	_____	B
1 per month minimum (9–17 for year)	_____	C
1 per 2 months minimum (4–8 for year)	_____	C-
less than 1 per 2 months (1–3 for year)	_____	D

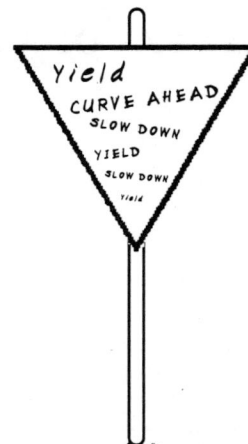

Vagabond Readers
©1997 F.P. Hendriks Publishing Ltd.
Permission to reproduce

Destinations—Correlation of Grades with Reading Goals

GRADE 8

Number of Books	Destination	Grade
5 per month minimum (45+ for year)	_____	A+
4 per month minimum (36–44 for year)	_____	A
3 per month minimum (27–35 for year)	_____	B
2 per month minimum (18–26 for year)	_____	C
1 per month minimum (9–17 for year)	_____	C-
less than 1 per month (1–8 for year)	_____	D

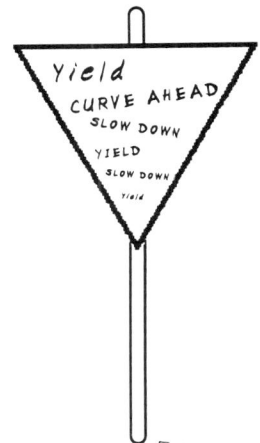

Yield
CURVE AHEAD
SLOW DOWN
YIELD
SLOW DOWN
Yield

Vagabond Readers
©1997 F.P. Hendriks Publishing Ltd.
Permission to reproduce

Destinations—Correlation of Grades with Reading Goals

GRADE 9

Number of Books	Destination	Grade
4 per month minimum (36+ for year)	_____	A+
3 per month minimum (27–35 for year)	_____	A
2 per month minimum (18–26 for year)	_____	B
1 per month minimum (9–17 for year)	_____	C
1 per 2 months minimum (4–8 for year)	_____	C-
less than 1 per 2 months (1–3 for year)	_____	D

Yield
CURVE AHEAD
SLOW DOWN
YIELD
SLOW DOWN

Destinations—Correlation of Grades with Reading Goals

GRADE _____

Number of Books	Destination	Grade
____ per month minimum (___+ for year)	_____	A+
___ per month minimum (___–___ for year)	_____	A
___ per month minimum (___–___ for year)	_____	B
___ per month minimum (___–___ for year)	_____	C
___ per ___ months minimum (___–___ for year)	_____	C-
less than ___ per ___ months (___–___ for year)	_____	D

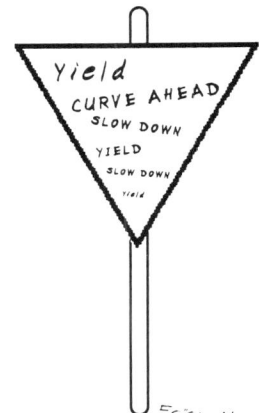

Yield
CURVE AHEAD
SLOW DOWN
YIELD
SLOW DOWN

Vagabond Readers
©1997 F.P. Hendriks Publishing Ltd.
Permission to reproduce

STUDENT PERFORMANCE MASTER

NAME _____

For Younger Readers

THINKING ABOUT CHOICES—Reading Survey

Directions: Read each question below carefully and then decide if you agree, if it doesn't apply to you, or if you disagree. Put a checkmark in one column to show your answer. There are no right or wrong answers to these questions but it is important that you answer honestly.

	Agree ✓	Does Not Apply ✓	Disagree ✓
When I am choosing a book from the library or choosing a book to buy:			
I think the cover of the book is very important.			
I read the back of the book jacket to help me to make a decision.			
I look for authors I have read before.			
The number of pages is important to me.			
I choose books that my friends are reading.			
I choose books that my friends have told me about.			
I prefer paperbacks.			
I prefer hardcover books.			
I ask for help to find books to read (e.g. librarian, card catalog)			
I just browse until I find a book I like.			
I read because I enjoy reading.			
I read because my teacher/parent wants me to read.			
Once I have chosen a book:			
I read it all the way through.			
I usually do not finish reading it.			
I read the ending first to find out what happens.			
I read the first page to decide if I want to read it.			
I finish the book and then decide if I liked it.			

For Older Readers

THINKING ABOUT CHOICES—Reading Survey

Directions: Read each question below carefully and then decide if you strongly agree, agree, if it doesn't apply to you, if you disagree, or if you strongly disagree. Put a checkmark in one column to show your answer. There are no right or wrong answers to these questions but it is important that you answer honestly.

	Strongly Agree ✓	Agree ✓	Does Not Apply ✓	Disagree ✓	Strongly Disagree ✓
When I am choosing a book from the library or choosing a book to buy:					
I think the cover of the book is very important.					
I read the back of the book jacket to help me make a decision.					
I look for authors I have read before.					
The number of pages is important to me.					
The size of the print is important to me.					
I choose books that my friends are reading.					
I choose books that my friends have told me about.					
I prefer paperbacks.					
I prefer hardcover books.					
I use a system to locate books (e.g. card catalog)					
I just browse until I find a book I like.					
I read because I am interested in reading.					
I read because my teacher/parent wants me to read.					
Once I have chosen a book:					
I read it all the way through.					
I always leave it unfinished.					
I read the ending first to find out what happens.					
I read the first page to decide if it is worth reading.					
I finish the book and then evaluate it.					

General Questions
LATITUDE FOR ATTITUDES—Reading Survey

Directions: Read each question and write your answer on the lines provided. There are no right or wrong answers but it is important that you answer honestly.

1. List the titles of the last three books that you read completely:

_____ _____ _____

2. How long does it generally take you to read one book of about 100–150 pages?

_____

3. Where do you usually read?

_____

_____

4. Does someone encourage you to read or do you choose to read on your own?

_____

_____

5. In what position do you read (sitting, lying down, at a desk, or on a bed or sofa)?

_____

6. What is the best story you have read? Explain.

_____

_____

7. What is the worst story you have read? Explain.

_____

_____

8. How important are each of the following in keeping your interest? Circle one for each.

	very important	moderately important	not important
action	1	2	3
description	1	2	3
characters	1	2	3
suspense	1	2	3

LATITUDE FOR ATTITUDES—Reading Survey, continued

9. What do you do when you come across unfamiliar words that you don't understand?

_____

_____

10. Have books influenced your life in any way? Explain.

_____

_____

11. Does anything interfere with your enjoyment of reading (how fast you read, how well you understand what you read, what books you have to choose from, sitting too close to friends, too much noise)?

_____

_____

12. What do you do about these obstacles?

_____

_____

13. Do you think reading will be more or less important to you twenty years from now? Explain.

_____

_____

14. Do you think there is any connection between reading ability and achievement in life? Explain.

_____

_____

For Younger Students

VAGABOND READER PASSPORT

Date:_____

GRADE _____
DECLARATION OF READING DESTINATION

I,_____,
    (Print name, first and last)

declare that I wish to travel to _____.
                                        (Print destination)

To make this trip, I will read_____books per month.

I will complete my reading journeys on or before _____.
                                                        (completion date.)

After finishing a book, I will hand in a log entry that shows that I understand the book. It will include all the information required by my teacher, and will be my own original work. I will correct any errors on the log entry as directed by my teacher. When my work is complete I will travel one unit toward my destination.

On reaching my destination and after participating in sharing activities and completing assigned exercises and projects, I understand that I will receive the grade of _____ which will be included in my final Language Arts mark.

Student Signature: _____

Parent/Guardian
Signature   _____

Teacher Signature   _____

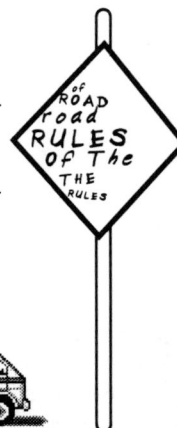

For Older Students

Date:_____

VAGABOND READER PASSPORT

GRADE _____

DECLARATION OF READING GOAL

I,_____,
      (Print name, first and last)

declare my intention to read _____books per month

between the present time and _____(completion date).

After finishing a book, I will submit a log entry that includes information about the book, its genre, and a bibliography. The log entry will be my own original work. I will make corrections as necessary until my submission meets what the teacher considers an acceptable standard.

On reaching my goal and after participating in sharing activities and completing assignments and projects, I understand that I will receive the grade of
_____which will be included in my final Language Arts mark.

Student Signature   _____

Parent/Guardian
Signature   _____

Teacher Signature   _____

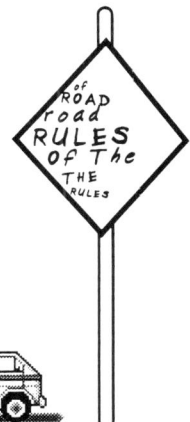

Making Reservations—Reader Awareness

If the students are to increase their experience of literature, then they must become aware of the reading habits they have already established. If students complete the reading survey provided in this chapter, then they may be encouraged to analyze or at least think about their own reading habits. However, this may be a difficult task for some students because many of the questions require the student to recall specific experiences and emotions of which they may not have been completely aware. The following lesson may be helpful for these students.

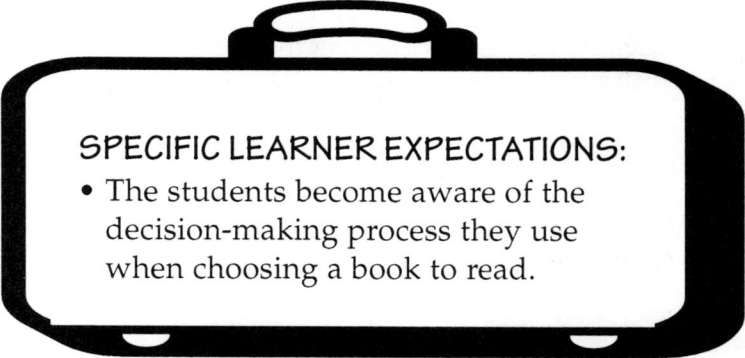

SPECIFIC LEARNER EXPECTATIONS:
- The students become aware of the decision-making process they use when choosing a book to read.

RESOURCES:
- a library with a selection of age-appropriate materials
- Student Performance Master "Booking for Vagabonds—Choosing a Book"

TEACHER:
- explains to the students that they are to choose a book from the library.
- directs students to concentrate on their actions and their reactions to certain books as they browse.

STUDENTS:
- choose a book.
- organize into small groups of three or four students to discuss questions on "Booking the Trip—Choosing a Book."
- record their answers.

TEACHER AND STUDENTS:
- discuss the students' answers to the questions.

Travel Insurance

Problems?
See Travel Insurance on page 10.

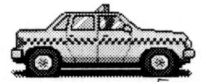

NAME _____

BOOKING FOR VAGABONDS—Choosing a Book

Directions: Answer the following questions on the lines provided. There are no right or wrong answers. Try to answer as honestly as possible.

1.   a) In what section of the library did you first look for a book? Why?

_____

_____

    b) Did you look in only one section of the library or did you look in two or more sections?

_____

_____

    c) Is this a good way to choose a book? Why?

_____

_____

2.   a) What part of the book did you look at first? (e.g. spine, cover, the first page...)

_____

_____

    b) Did you find the book right away or did you return to it after looking at other books?

_____

_____

    c) Is this a good way to choose a book? Why?

_____

_____

3.   a) Did you read any part of the book (including the back cover) before you chose it? Why or why not?

_____

_____

BOOKING FOR VAGABONDS—Choosing a Book, continued

b) Is this a good way to evaluate a story?

_____

_____

c) What are some other ways of evaluating whether a book would be worthwhile to read?

_____

_____

4. a) What type of book did you choose to read? Is this the type of book you usually read or is it a different type of book? Explain.

_____

_____

b) Who is the author of your book? Name other books you have read by this author, if any.

_____

_____

c) Did you choose the book because a friend recommended it or do you prefer to choose books independently?

_____

_____

d) Which of these do you think is a good way to choose a book? Explain.

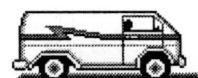

_____

_____

Chapter Two: Knowing How to Navigate

Heading in the "Write" Direction

Kori: Now that the students have chosen their reading destinations and signed their passports, they're due for a few lessons in navigation.

Heather: I agree. They need directions and practice in identifying and locating the various resources that are available at our "travel agency."

Kori: In order to d o that, the students must be able to use the library catalog. They could think of it as a travel guide.

Heather: Each traveler should also be able to show his or her route by means of a bibliography—flight plan.

Kori: And finally, students must be prepared to log their experiences in literature. Their log books will link their reading achievements to the writing process.

Heather: Each completed log entry will be an indication that the student is getting closer to his or her destination.

Spying Out the Options—Introduction to Library Organization

In order to feel confident as they begin to search for materials in the library/travel agency, students need opportunities to investigate the types of resources found in the various areas and to discover how these are organized. This overview lesson provides a foundation for further development of the students' navigating skills.

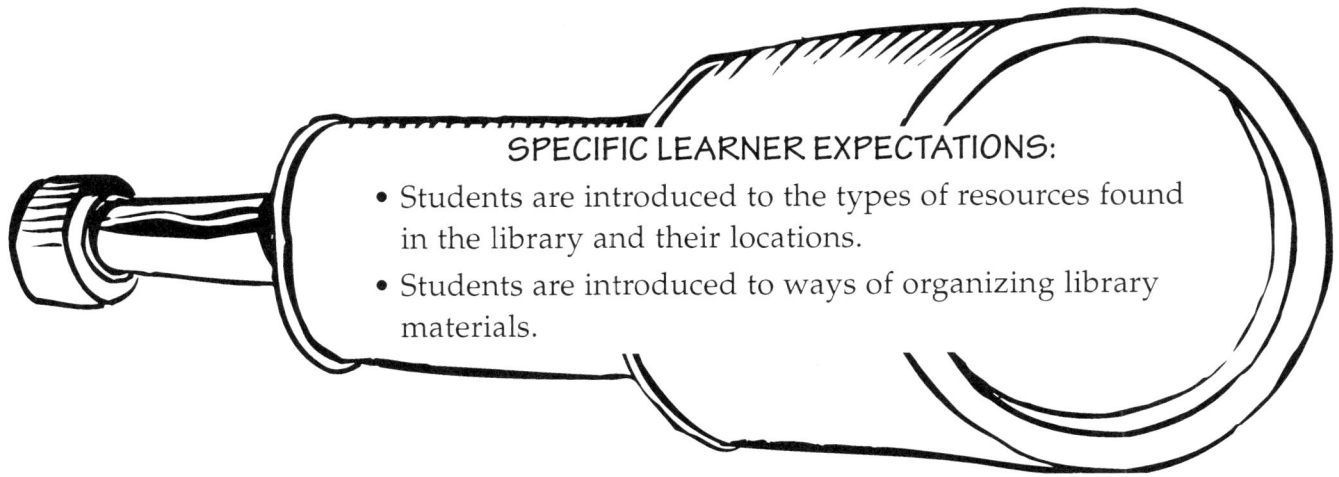

SPECIFIC LEARNER EXPECTATIONS:

- Students are introduced to the types of resources found in the library and their locations.
- Students are introduced to ways of organizing library materials.

RESOURCES:

- the library and its signs
- the librarian
- various library resources
- Student Performance Master "Travel Agency Map" (intended for Younger Readers)

TEACHER AND/OR LIBRARIAN:

- points out or reviews the location in the library of the following areas:

Atlases	Encyclopedias on CD-ROM
Audio-Visual Materials	Fiction
Biographies	General References
Card or Computerized Catalog	Newspapers
Circulation Desk	Nonfiction
Dictionaries	Periodicals
Encyclopedias	Vertical File

- provides one or two examples of the resources found in each area.

Teacher, continued

- indicates how the materials in each area are organized.

Examples:

Biographies: arranged by call number consisting of the letter B plus first three letters of author's surname or by call number consisting of Dewey decimal (920 or 921) plus first three letters of author's surname

Encyclopedias: arranged numerically by volume

Fiction: arranged by call number consisting of the letter F plus first three letters of author's surname

General Reference: arranged by call number

Nonfiction: arranged by call number consisting of Dewey decimal plus first three letters of author's surname

Periodicals: filed alphabetically; current issues placed on display

Vertical File: filed alphabetically

STUDENTS:

- complete Student Performance Master "Travel Agency Map" (Younger Readers).

        OR

- draw a diagram of the library labeling the location of the various areas. This activity is intended for older students and can be done individually, in pairs, or in groups of three.

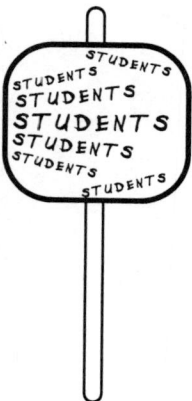

TRAVEL AGENCY MAP

Directions: Create an imaginative name for your library. Write it on the line below.

_____ Travel Agency

Use a sheet of paper to draw a map of your travel agency/library. Illustrate and label as many of the following locations as possible:

ATLAS Avenue

AUDIO-VISUAL Alley

BIOGRAPHY Boulevard

CARD/COMPUTER CATALOG Court

CD-pROMenade

CIRCULATION Station

DICTIONARY Drive

ENCYCLOPEDIA Estates

HARDCOVER FICTION Highway

LEGEND and FABLE Lane

NONFICTION Neighborhood

NEWSPAPER Nexus

PAPERBACK FICTION Park

PERIODICAL Passage

REFERENCE Road

VERTICAL FILE Valley

Wayfarer's Walkabout—Library Organization Follow-up

This lesson reinforces what students learned in the previous one and gives them an opportunity to demonstrate their knowledge of "what goes where" in the library/travel agency.

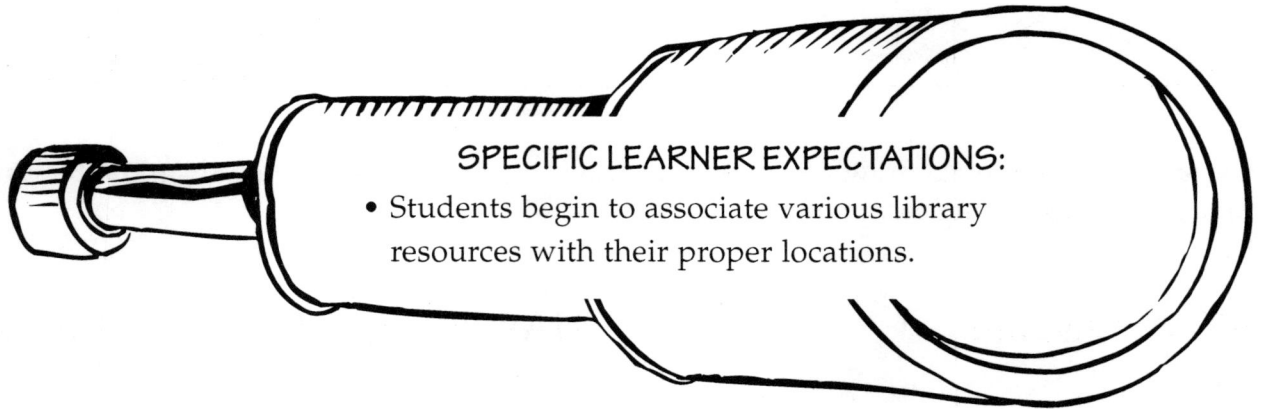

SPECIFIC LEARNER EXPECTATIONS:

- Students begin to associate various library resources with their proper locations.

RESOURCES:

- a variety of library materials from different areas or departments.
- Student Performance Master "Travel Guide"

TEACHER AND/OR LIBRARIAN:

- preselects one or two items from each of the various areas of the library.
- shows the items to the class in random order and asks students where each belongs.

TEACHER AND STUDENTS:

- return the items to their proper area as each is identified.

SIGNPOST:

The librarian may prefer that students do not actually re-shelve or file the items, but place them in front of where they belong.

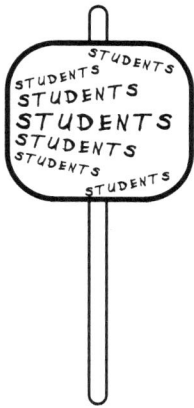

STUDENTS:

- group themselves in pairs to complete the following:

  1. One student describes an item or resource found in the library, giving its name and/or make-believe title as well as an example of the kind of information the resource might provide.

  2. The other student then names the area where the item would be located, based on his or her partner's description.

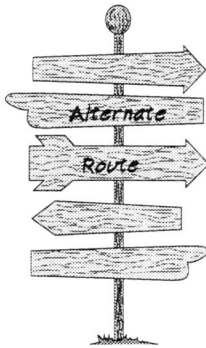

ALTERNATE ROUTE:

If preferred, the introductory part of the lesson may be modified as follows:

1. **Teacher** distributes a list of the various library areas to the class.

   Atlases

   Audio-visual Materials

   Biographies

   Card or Computerized Catalog

   Circulation Desk

   Dictionaries

   Encyclopedias

   Encyclopedias on CD-ROM

   Fiction

   General References

   Newspapers

   Nonfiction

   Periodicals

   Vertical File

2. **Students** match the items held up by the teacher to the areas on the list.

   This can be an oral activity or a pen and paper activity.

Resource Relay—A Game for Younger Readers

This is a fun relay for elementary students to practice finding various types of resources in the travel agency/library.

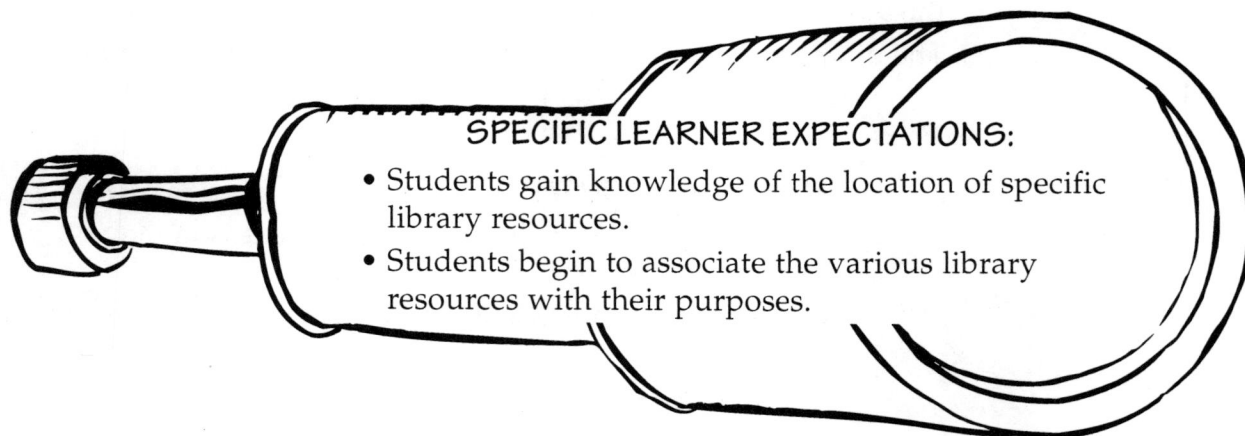

SPECIFIC LEARNER EXPECTATIONS:

- Students gain knowledge of the location of specific library resources.
- Students begin to associate the various library resources with their purposes.

RESOURCES:

- Student Performance Master "Resource Quests"
- Student Performance Master "Searchmobile"
- boxes, hats, envelopes, or other containers equal to the number of teams

TEACHER:

- divides class into two teams of ten to fifteen students each.
- photocopies "Searchmobile" master, one for each team.
- photocopies "Resource Quests" master and cuts apart the items on each copy.
- supplies each team with a set of quests (equal to the number of team members) in a box, hat, or envelope.
- cuts each team's "Searchmobile" master into puzzle-like pieces, with the number of pieces equal to the number of team members.
- directs the relay, presenting each student with a piece of the "Searchmobile" puzzle as he or she successfully completes a quest.

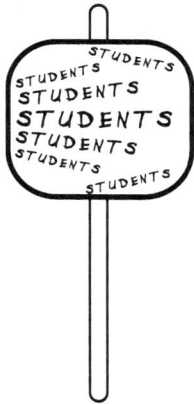

STUDENTS:

- line up in random order in teams.
- follow these directions:
    1. The first student on each team selects a quest from the hat.
    2. After locating the required resource, he or she brings it to the teacher.
    3. If the quest was successful, the teacher gives the student a piece of the "Searchmobile" puzzle.
    4. The student returns to her or his team with the puzzle piece and the next member of the team proceeds with a new quest.
    5. Team members who have completed their quests work at putting the puzzle pieces together.
    6. Team members may return the quest to the box and forfeit a turn if they are having difficulty.
    7. The team that completes all quests and completes the puzzle wins the relay.

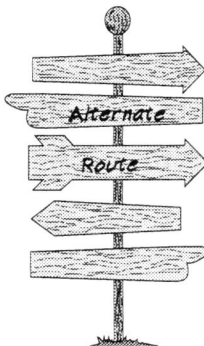

ALTERNATE ROUTE:

If preferred, the "Resource Quests" master may be used for a scavenger hunt:

1. Divide the class into two, three, or four equal teams.
2. Teams receive their puzzle pieces after they complete **all** the quests and give the appropriate items to the teacher.
3. As in the relay, the first team to complete the "Searchmobile" puzzle is the winner.

RESOURCE QUESTS

NAME_____

Find a book with a call number beginning with the Dewey decimal 796.

Find a book by an author whose last name begins with R.

Find an encyclopedia volume that contains information about the moon.

Find a magazine that contains a picture of an animal.

Find a book that contains a picture of a person.

Find a book that has the word mystery in its title.

Find a resource that contains current information about world leaders.

Find an audio, video, pamphlet, or vertical file resource about the environment.

Find a resource that contains a map of Africa.

Find a resource that can be used to find the meaning of the word lapidary.

Find a book that contains a myth, legend, fable, or folk tale.

Find a newspaper that contains a letter to the editor.

Find a book that tells the story of a famous person's life.

Find a book that contains poems or nursery rhymes.

Find a magazine that contains an article you would be interested in reading.

SEARCHMOBILE

NAME_____

Vagabond Readers
©1997 F.P. Hendriks Publishing Ltd.
Permission to reproduce

Gold-panning in Resource River—Finding Answers for Older Readers

As they explore the library, forming questions and "mining" resources for appropriate answers, junior high school students will gain a better appreciation of the wealth of information that is available to them.

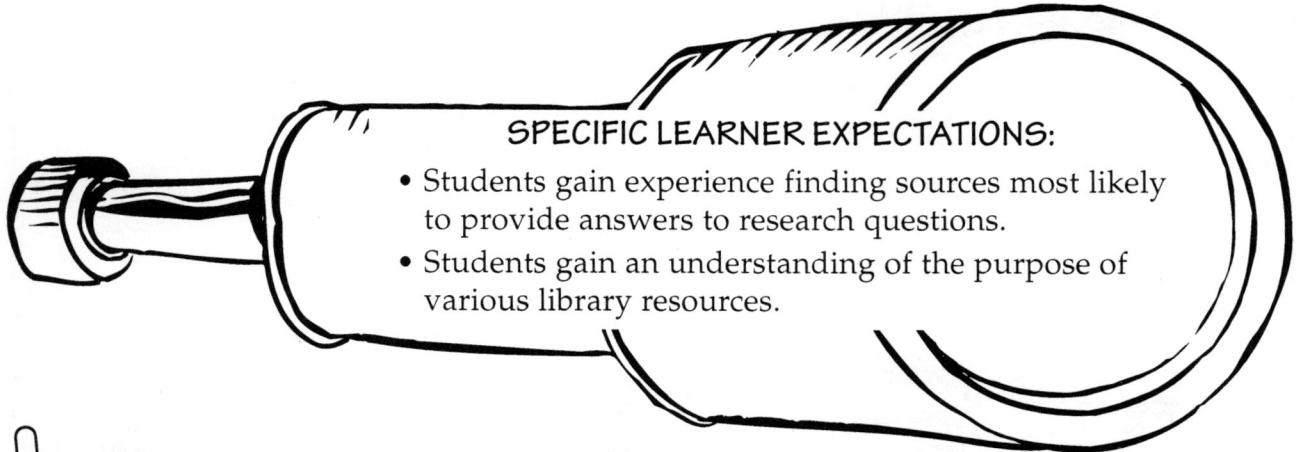

SPECIFIC LEARNER EXPECTATIONS:

- Students gain experience finding sources most likely to provide answers to research questions.
- Students gain an understanding of the purpose of various library resources.

RESOURCES:

- various library resources
- 5 x 8-inch index cards

TEACHER:

- prepares in advance a set of index cards (one for every group of two or three students). Each card is numbered on one side (beginning at 1) and has the name of an area in the library on the other side.
- divides the class into groups of two or three and gives each group three blank cards.

STUDENTS:

- follow directions:

    1. Each group labels one blank card PAN and a second card NUGGETS.
    2. Group members each select one of the numbered cards that have been placed in a pile with numbered sides up.
    3. Individuals find the library area listed on the back of the card selected.
    4. Each group develops two to five questions (depending on the time available) that can be answered using the resources in that area. A time limit may be given, e.g. ten minutes.

Students, continued

5. They record their questions on the PAN card. This card remains in the area.

6. They record the answers to the questions they have developed, along with their precise location (including title, volume, and page number) on the card labeled NUGGETS and give it to the teacher.

7. After a set amount of time, e.g. five minutes, groups carousel (rotate) from one area to the next (those in area 1 go to area 2, and so on).

8. Each group answers the questions developed by the original group and records these answers on the third blank card.

9. When all groups have completed the circuit, they compare their answers to those on the NUGGET cards held by the teacher to see which groups were most successful in finding answers.

SIGN POST:

Depending on the age of the students and the number of students in each group, it may be helpful if one group member group stays behind to encourage and/or provide assistance to the groups searching for answers. This student could then be in charge of the NUGGET card, instead of the teacher). In this way, the groups answering the questions get immediate feedback on their answers.

Managing the Guide—Card/Computer Catalogs

To search for a particular resource, students must be able to use the travel guide, whether it is a computerized catalog or a card system. Understanding the information in a catalog entry will help students to find an item and also help them to decide if a particular book is likely to contain the information they need.

SPECIFIC LEARNER EXPECTATIONS:

- Students use the information they find in the card catalog or computerized catalog.

RESOURCES:

- Overhead Projection "Card Catalog Samples"
- Student Performance Master "Compass Challenge" (for Younger Readers)
- Student Reference "Two Types of Travel Guides"

TEACHER OR LIBRARIAN:

- uses Student Reference "Two Types of Travel Guides" to provide basic information on the type of catalog found in the library.
- uses either the sample cards on the Overhead Projection Master "Card Catalog Samples" or the appropriate computer screen to identify each component of the catalog entry, including:

Call Number	Physical Description
Body	- Pages
- Author	- Illustrations
- Title	- Size
- Series	**International Standard Book Number (ISBN)**
- Place of Publication	**Added Entry section** (lists the headings on
- Publisher	other entries for the same item)
- Date of Publication or Copyright	

STUDENTS:

- complete Student Performance Master "Compass Challenge" (for younger students).
   OR
- locate a book in the library after recording the required information from the catalog (for older students).

Card Catalog Samples

AUTHOR CARD

F	Halvorson, Marilyn
HAL	Brothers and strangers. Toronto: Stoddart, ©1991.
	181pp. 20cm.
	I. Title

ISBN 0-7737-5369-9

TITLE CARD

	The disappearing bike shop
F	Woodruff, Elvira
WOO	The disappearing bike shop. New York: Bantam Doubleday Dell, ©1992.
	169pp. 20cm.
	I. Title

ISBN 0-440-40938-1

Vagabond Readers
©1997 F.P. Hendriks Publishing Ltd.
Permission to reproduce

Card Catalog Samples

SUBJECT CARD

CREATIVE WRITING

808	Hearn, Emily
068	Draw and write your own picture book.
HEA	(Storyboarding).

Markham: Pembroke Publishers, ©1990.

   32pp. 20cm. illus.

1. Creative writing.

I. Thurman, Mark

II. Title

III. Series: Storyboarding

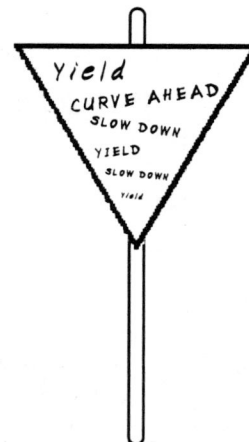

COMPASS CHALLENGE

Directions: Use the information you find about a particular book in the card or computer catalog to complete the compass diagram. Trade diagrams with another student and use your fellow traveler's compass heading to locate the book he or she has identified.

Title

_____

Author

_____

Call Number

_____

_____

_____

TWO TYPES OF TRAVEL GUIDES

1. ## Card Catalog

- Books are listed alphabetically in the card catalog under their title, author, and subject.

- There may be three or more cards in the card catalog for a particular book. The cards are duplicates except for their headings.

- One card, giving the author's name at the top, serves as the basis for all other cards that describe a particular book. This card is called the **main entry**. The other cards for that book, which appear with additional headings (i.e. appropriate subject headings, or the book's title) are called **added entries**.

- The **call number** in the upper left hand corner of the card indicates the book's classification and placement on the shelves. The call number for a fiction (story) book usually consists of the letter **F** followed by the first three letters of the author's surname. The call number for a nonfiction book consists of a subject classification number (i.e. Dewey decimal) followed by the first three letters of the author's surname.

2. ## Computerized Catalog

- To search for a book, the user is instructed to enter one of the following: title, author, subject, or keyword.

- After the search word is entered, the computer searches its files and provides a list of applicable titles along with their call numbers. Usually it also indicates if the books are in or out on loan.

- Most computer catalogs provide the same information that is found on a catalog card although it may be arranged in a different format.

Bibliographies—The "Why" Lesson

Bibliographies are compiled on certain subjects, time periods, or authors. The content of a bibliography depends on the bibliographer's purpose. The following activity is designed to help the students develop their own understanding of the reasons for compiling a bibliography.

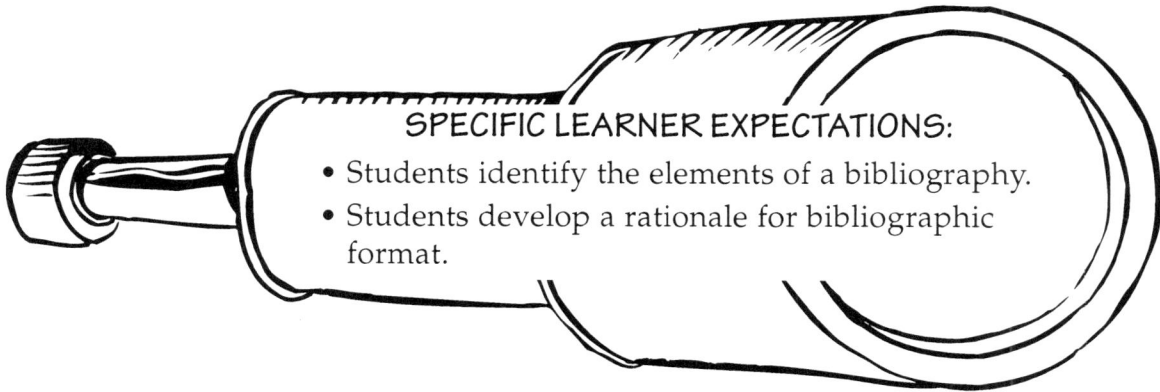

SPECIFIC LEARNER EXPECTATIONS:

- Students identify the elements of a bibliography.
- Students develop a rationale for bibliographic format.

RESOURCES:

- Student Performance Master "Why Bibliographies?"
- local phone books for each group of students
- sample tenant list from an apartment complex
- any other document listing surnames first
- encyclopedias of the same name but with different years of publication

TEACHER:

- explains what a bibliography is and its purpose.
- discusses the instructions for the Student Performance Master "Why Bibliographies?" with the students.
- displays the resources provided and discusses their purposes, both individually and in general (reference, obtaining information).

STUDENTS:

- in groups of two or three, complete the Student Performance Master "Why Bibliographies?"

TEACHER AND STUDENTS:

- discuss students' answers to the questions.
- draw conclusions on why bibliographies are set up in this way.
- discuss other uses for bibliographies (academic work, nonfiction books).

WHY BIBLIOGRAPHIES?

Directions: Discuss the following questions in your group and record your responses on the lines provided.

1. Examine your sample phone book, tenant list, or other resources provided.

    a) How are the names arranged in each?

_____

_____

    b) Which name (first or last) do you look for when trying to locate an entry?

_____

_____

    c) Why do you think that name is used rather than the other?

_____

_____

    d) Do bibliographies use this same method for author names? Why or Why not?

_____

_____

2. List three places where you have seen words or phrases underlined or italicized.

    a) Why do you think underlining or italicizing is used?

_____

_____

    b) What would be the purpose of underlining or italicizing in bibliographies?

_____

_____

3. Look at the two encyclopedias.

    a) If you had only the bibliography for the two, how could you tell them apart?

_____

_____

    b) Which encyclopedia would you choose to get the most current information? Why?

_____

_____

    c) What information in a bibliography helps you to distinguish between encyclopedias with the same title?

_____

_____

    d) What are some reasons for including the publisher and the city in a bibliography?

_____

_____

Recording Reading Routes (for Younger Readers)

In this lesson, elementary students are introduced to the bibliographic elements that can help others who may want to "follow in their footsteps." Students use this information to identify a particular book they have been reading.

SPECIFIC LEARNER EXPECTATIONS:

- Students are introduced to some of the bibliographic elements that help to identify a particular book.
- Students practice recording these elements.

RESOURCES:

- Student Performance Master "Biblio-bridging"
- fiction books from the library

TEACHER:

- introduces or reviews the elements of a bibliography: author, title, place of publication (city), publisher, and copyright year
- reminds students that a record of this information helps others to "track" the reader's journey.
- presents the mnemonic device "**A**nother **t**raveler **c**an **p**ursue **y**ou." This helps students remember the five elements (**a**uthor, **t**itle, **c**ity, **p**ublisher, **y**ear).
- shows students where bibliographic information is found, using one or two examples from the library.

STUDENTS:

- complete Student Performance Master "Biblio-Bridging."

SIGN POST:

An added benefit of using the suggested mnemonic device is that students will learn the elements in the order in which they will eventually record them in a bibliography.

STUDENT PERFORMANCE MASTER

NAME_____

BIBLIO-BRIDGING

Directions: Using the fiction book you are reading, find the:

- author
- title
- city
- publisher
- copyright year

Record this information in the appropriate blanks on your "biblio-bridge." Remember the statement "**A**nother **t**raveler **c**an **p**ursue **y**ou." It may help you to recall the required elements.

T_____
　　Title

C_____
　　City

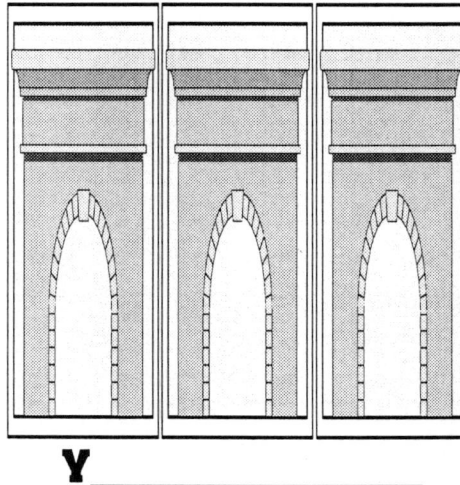

A_____
　　Author

Y_____
　　Year

P_____
　　Publisher

Another traveler can pursue you!

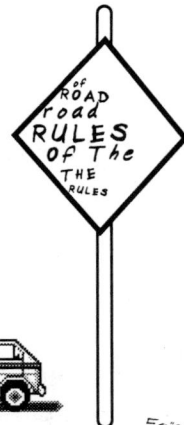

Vagabond Readers
©1997 F.P. Hendriks Publishing Ltd.
Permission to reproduce

Recording Reading Routes (for Older Readers)

This lesson helps junior high/middle school students identify the various elements used in a bibliography and makes them aware of the mechanics and format to be used when recording their own bibliographies/reading routes.

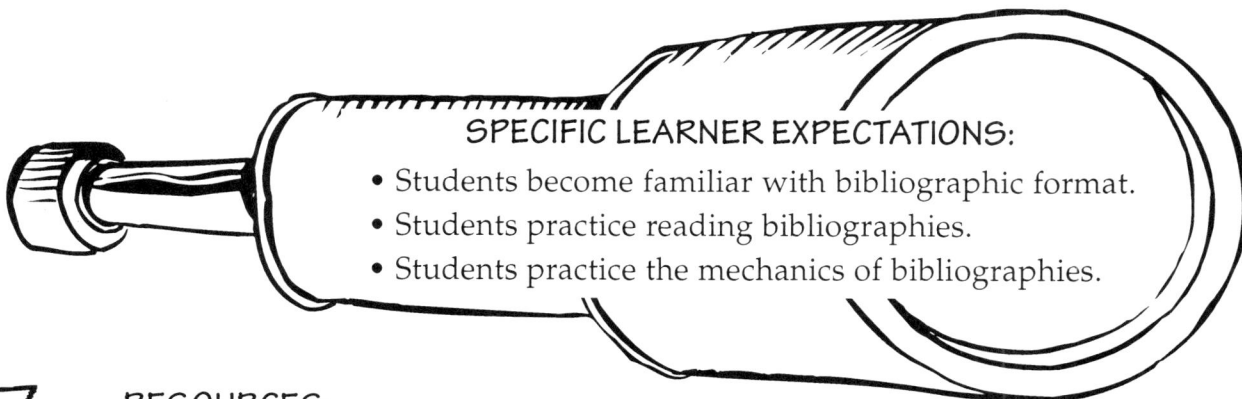

SPECIFIC LEARNER EXPECTATIONS:

- Students become familiar with bibliographic format.
- Students practice reading bibliographies.
- Students practice the mechanics of bibliographies.

RESOURCES:

- Overhead Projections "Mechanical Matters, Parts 1 and 2"
- Student Performance Master "Graphing a Path"
- Student Reference "Bibliographic Format"

TEACHER:

- introduces or reviews the concept of a bibliography (a list of resources).
- reviews elements of a bibliography: author, title, place of publication (city), publisher, copyright year.
- compares a bibliographic record to a flight path, reminding students that the information in the record helps others track/follow the reader's journey.
- uses Student Reference "Bibliographic Format" to briefly discuss the similarities and differences in bibliographic formats depending on the source.

TEACHER AND STUDENTS:

- answer questions on Overhead Projections "Mechanical Matters, Parts 1 and 2."

STUDENTS:

- complete Student Performance Master "Graphing a Path."

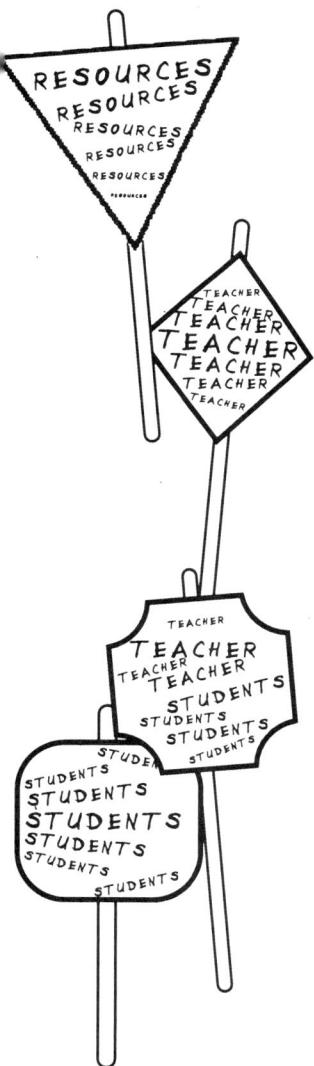

SIGN POST:

Answer sheets for the Overhead Projections "Mechanical Matters, Parts 1 and 2 and the Student Performance Master "Graphing a Path" are found in the Appendix on pages 149–151.

Mechanical Matters, Part 1

Bibliography

Choyce, Lesley. *Good Idea Gone Bad**. Halifax, NS: Formac, 1993.

Mackay, Claire. *The Minerva Program*. Toronto, ON: James Lorimer, 1984.

Rinaldi, Ann. *The Last Silk Dress*. New York: Bantam, 1988.

Wells, Rosemary. *When No One Was Looking*. New York: Scholastic, 1980.

Use the bibliography above to complete:

1. The publisher of *The Last Silk Dress* is

   _____.

2. The author of *The Minerva Program* is

   _____.

3. Scholastic published a book by Rosemary Wells in the year _____.

4. The book by Lesley Choyce was published in the city of _____.

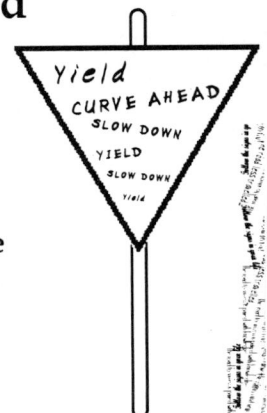

*Book titles are generally identified using italics, and where italics are not possible, by underlining.

Mechanical Matters, Part 2

Insert punctuation as required:

1. Christopher Matt *Wingman on Ice* Boston MA: Little Brown & Co 1964

2. Bennett Jay *The Skeleton Man* New York Ballantine 1986

3. Jacobs Paul Samuel *Born into Light* New York Scholastic 1988

Insert punctuation, underline,* and capitalize as required. Write the entry on the line below:

4. hunt irene up a road slowly new york berkley 1966

    _____

5. beagle peter s the last unicorn new york ballantine 1968

    _____

6. Frank B. Gilbreth, Jr. and Ernestine Gilbreth Carey, a brother and sister, co-authored a book entitled *Cheaper by the Dozen*. It was copyrighted in 1948 and published in Toronto by Bantam Books. Write a bibliographic entry for this book.

    _____

    _____

    _____

*Book titles are generally identified using italics, and where italics are not possible, by underlining.

Vagabond Readers
©1997 F.P. Hendriks Publishing Ltd.
Permission to reproduce

GRAPHING A PATH

NAME_____

Use the following bibliography to answer the questions below.

Bibliography

Hughes, Monica. *My Name is Paula Popowich!** Toronto, ON: James Lorimer, 1983.
Naylor, Phyllis Reynolds. *The Keeper*. Toronto, ON: Bantam, 1986.
Peck, Richard. *Remembering the Good Times*. New York: Dell, 1985.
Snyder, Carol. *The Leftover Kid*. New York: Berkley, 1986.

---

1. The publisher of *Remembering the Good Times* is _____.

2. Naylor's book was published in the city of _____

   by _____.

3. The author of *The Leftover Kid* is _____.

4. The book by Monica Hughes was published in the year _____.

5. Insert the correct punctuation for the following two books:

   Callahan Steven Adrift New York Ballantine 1986

   Nelson O T The Girl Who Owned a City New York Dell 1975

6. Rewrite the following bibliographic entry. Insert punctuation, underline, and capitalize as required.

   paulsen gary the crossing new york orchard 1987

   _____

   _____

8. Write a bibliographic entry for Victoria M. Althoff's book entitled *Key to My Heart*, published in 1989 by Willowisp Press of Worthington, Ohio.

   _____

   _____

*Book titles are generally identified using italics, and where italics are not possible, by underlining.

BIBLIOGRAPHIC FORMAT

A. Book, one author

Kassem, Lou. *The Treasures of Witch Hat Mountain.** New York: Avon, 1992.

B. Book, two or more authors

Bankhead, Elizabeth, Carole Martinez, Janet Nichols, and Ruth Anne Windmiller. *Write It: A Guide for Research.** Englewood, CO: Libraries Unlimited, 1988.

C. Article from a periodical or encyclopedia

Kimball, Gayle. "How to Ace Your Classes." *Teen.** August 1995, p. 62.

Radwin, Eugene. "Literacy and Illiteracy." *Grolier Academic Encyclopedia.** New York: Grolier International, 1991.

D. Newspaper article

Caster, Penny. "An Artist Who Really Talks Turkey." *The Red Deer Advocate.** 13 January 1996, Sec. C, p. 1.

E. A book or article with no author given

"Architecture." *The Junior Encyclopedia of Canada.** Edmonton, AB: Hurtig, 1990. 1:81–87.

F. Pamphlet

De Bruyn, Robert L. "The Different Hats You Wear Can Help Your Teaching." *The Master Teacher.** Vol. 24, No. 7. Manhattan, KN: Leadership Lane, 19 October, 1992.

G. CD-ROM

"Children's Literature." *Microsoft Encarta.** 1996 ed. CD-ROM. Redmond: Microsoft, 1996.

H. Internet

Middleton, Don. "American Black Bears." *The Bear Den.* 21 Jan. 1996. Available: http://www.nature-net.com/bears/black.

*Book titles are generally identified using italics, and where italics are not possible, by underlining.

Vagabond Readers
©1997 F.P. Hendriks Publishing Ltd.
Permission to reproduce

Logging Miles with the Novel Summary

Students will find the novel summary a useful tool to begin logging their reading accomplishments. This lesson provides a structure for them to follow while enabling the teacher to assess reading comprehension and writing skills early in the year.

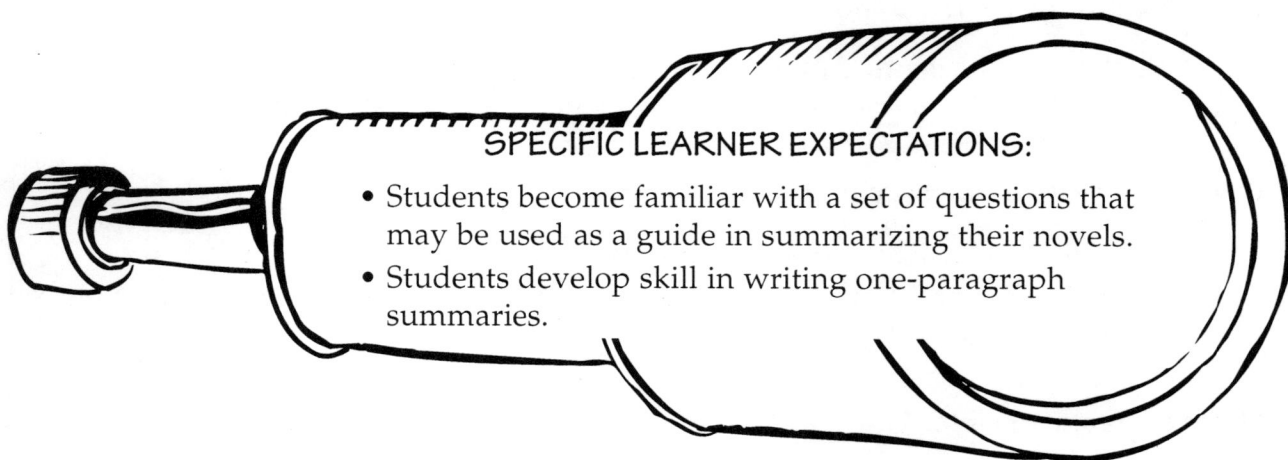

SPECIFIC LEARNER EXPECTATIONS:

- Students become familiar with a set of questions that may be used as a guide in summarizing their novels.
- Students develop skill in writing one-paragraph summaries.

RESOURCES:

- Student Reference "The 5–W System for Summarizing Novels" (for Younger Readers)
- Student Reference "The 7–What System for Summarizing Novels" (for Older Readers)
- a familiar fairy tale of the teacher's or students' choice
- a "Novel Summary" log entry card (or sheet) for each student with the appropriate "Bibliography" format on the reverse.

TEACHER:

- reads age-appropriate Student Reference orally with students and explains each question to be answered.
- stresses that in order to be accepted as a log entry, each summary must contain at least seven informative points.
- reads fairy tale aloud to the students.

TEACHER AND STUDENTS:

- in small groups, write a one-paragraph summary of the fairy tale using the Student Reference as a guide.
- share the summaries with other groups.

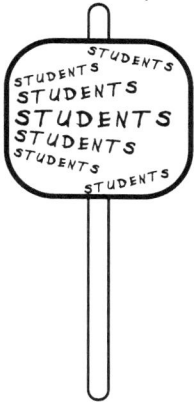

STUDENTS:

- read another short story independently.
- write a summary for that story in the appropriate space on a Novel Summary log entry card.
- record "reading route" on the back of the card. Teachers may wish to have younger readers construct a biblio-bridge, while older readers may be asked for a complete bibliographic entry.

SIGN POST:

After completing their individual log entries, the students may attach them to their card-holders or travel logs. These example cards will then be available to each student to use as a reference when he or she begins to complete log entries for novels. The classification section below the Reading Route may be left blank until the lesson on forms of literature has been completed. (See "Company Characteristics, pages 94–95")

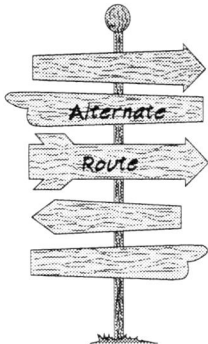

ALTERNATE ROUTE:

Students use felt pens to write the group's one-paragraph summary of the fairy tale on large chart paper. Post these around the room. Other groups then "carousel" (rotate) around the room reading all the summaries and noting how they are the same or different from their own.

THE 5–W SYSTEM FOR SUMMARIZING NOVELS

A **novel summary** is a short outline of the story. Answering the following questions about your novel will help you to write a summary paragraph. You may use the answer to either **#1** or **#2** to begin your paragraph. The answer to either of the questions in **#5** may be used to end your paragraph.

Questions

1.   **Where** does the story take place?

2.   **When** does the story occur?

3.   **Who** are the main characters (i.e. the characters most important to the story)?

4.   **What** do the main characters want?

   and

   What problem must the characters solve?

5.   **Why** did you or did you not like the story?

   and

   Why would you or would you not recommend this book to a friend?

Keep in mind:

A.   Your summary must include seven different points about the book in order to be acceptable as a log entry. This means that you must answer all seven questions, including both **whats** and both **whys**.

B.   You do not need to combine the elements in the order suggested, but your paragraph should have a definite beginning and ending.

C.   Try to make your paragraph interesting to the reader.

D.   Do not give away the surprises or the story's ending!

THE 7–WHAT SYSTEM FOR SUMMARIZING NOVELS

A **novel summary** is a brief outline of the story. It should convey, in a sentence, the novel's theme or meaning and briefly show how the theme is developed by the author.

Answering the following questions about your novel will help you to write a summary paragraph. The answer to **#1** may be your **topic sentence**. The answer to **#7** may be your **concluding sentence**. The other answers provide supporting details.

Memorizing the statement **THESE STORIES CREATE GATEWAYS AROUND OUR LIBRARY** can help you to remember the seven questions.

Questions

1. What **theme** or main idea was the author trying to get across in this story?

2. What **situation** does the author set up in order to get across the theme or main idea?

3. What are the names of the **characters** who are involved in this situation?

4. What is the main character's **goal** or motivation?

5. What **action** does the main character take in order to deal with the situation?

6. What **obstacle(s)** must be overcome in order for the main character to achieve his or her goal?

7. What did you **like** best about this book?

> ### Keep in mind:
>
> A.   Your summary must include seven different points about the book in order to be acceptable as a log entry. This means that you must answer all seven questions or give other information that you feel is important.
>
> B.   You do not necessarily need to combine the elements in the order suggested, but your paragraph should have a definite topic sentence, supporting details, and a concluding sentence.
>
> C.   Be brief, but try to build interest in the story.
>
> D.   Do not give away any surprises or the story's ending!

NOVEL SUMMARY

Requirement: 7 points in paragraph form

Name: _____

Class: _____

Title: _____

Author: _____

Answer: Where? When? Who? What do the main characters want? What problem must be solved? Why did you or did you not like the book? Why would you or would you not recommend it to a friend?

_____

_____

_____

_____

_____

_____

_____

✂ -

NOVEL SUMMARY

Requirement: 7 points in paragraph form

Name: _____

Class: _____

Title: _____

Author: _____

Consider: **T**heme, **S**ituation, **C**haracters, **G**oals, **A**ctions taken, **O**bstacles overcome. Also tell what you **l**iked best. Remember THESE STORIES CREATE GATEWAYS AROUND OUR LIBRARY.

_____

_____

_____

_____

_____

_____

READING ROUTE / BIBLIOGRAPHY

_____

_____

_____

TRAVEL COMPANY / CLASSIFICATION (check one)

_____ Briney's Shipping: BIOGRAPHY

_____ Mega-rapid Air and Rail: MODERN REALISTIC

_____ Hustler's Stagecoach: HISTORICAL

_____ Feather Landing Winged Chariots: FOLKLORE

_____ Fringe's Magic Carpets: FANTASY

_____ Space Flyer Intergalactic Express: SCIENCE FICTION

BIBLIOGRAPHY

_____

_____

_____

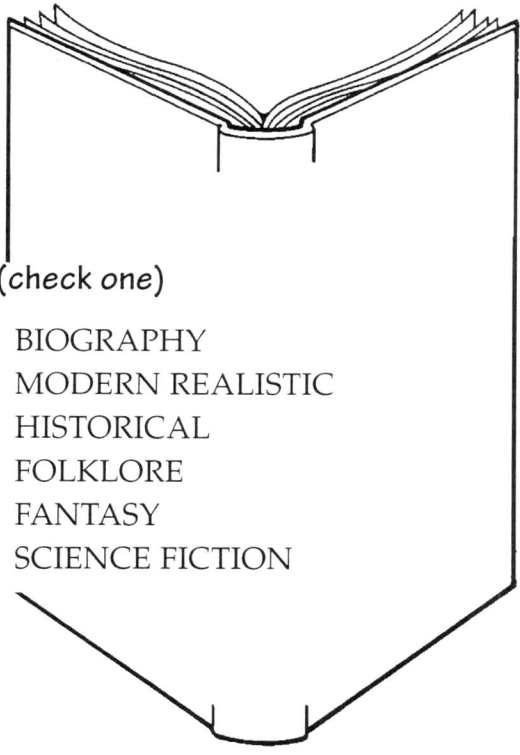

CLASSIFICATION (check one)

_____ BIOGRAPHY

_____ MODERN REALISTIC

_____ HISTORICAL

_____ FOLKLORE

_____ FANTASY

_____ SCIENCE FICTION

Completing Log Entries in Other Formats

Students are introduced to other formats for logging their reading journeys.

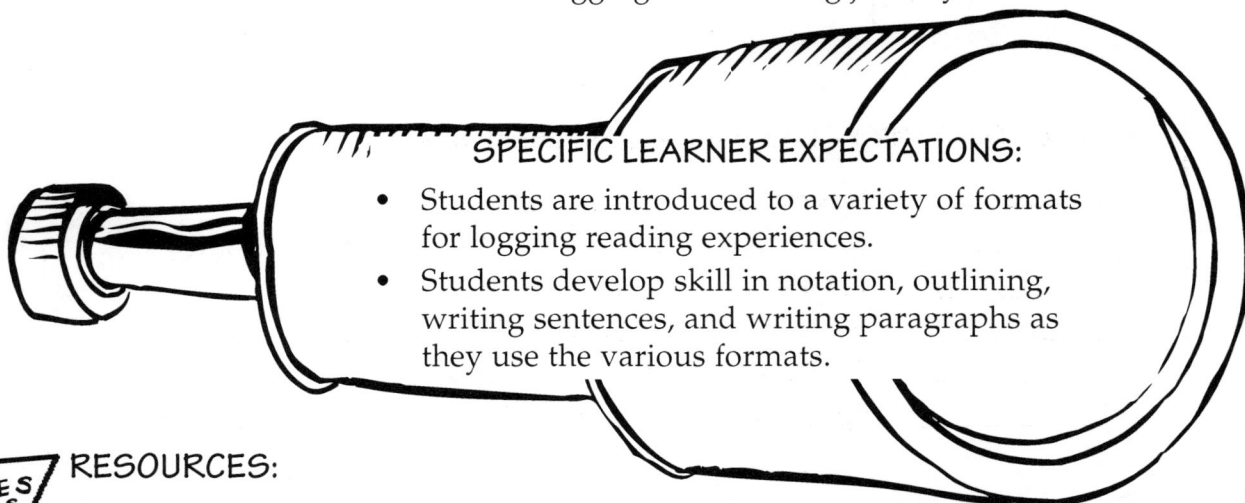

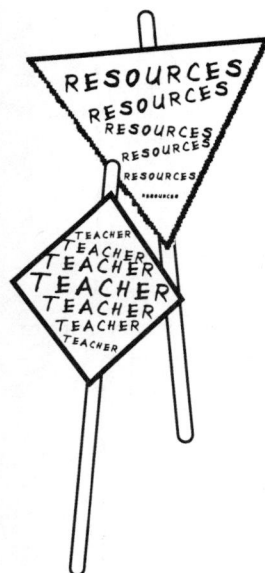

SPECIFIC LEARNER EXPECTATIONS:

- Students are introduced to a variety of formats for logging reading experiences.
- Students develop skill in notation, outlining, writing sentences, and writing paragraphs as they use the various formats.

RESOURCES:

- Teacher Reference "Novel Summary Assessment," pages 73, 75, 77, and 79
- other formats for log entries, pages 74, 76, 78, and 80

TEACHER:

- discusses the procedure for completing each type of log entry.
- notes that in addition to supplying information about the story, students will be required to record their "reading route" by means of a biblio-bridge for younger readers or a complete bibliographic entry for older readers.
- indicates that students will learn how to complete the classification section at a later date.
- reviews the minimum information requirement for each format as discussed in the previous lesson: seven points in complete sentences or fourteen points in notes or point form.

TEACHER AND STUDENTS:

- discuss and/or review, as necessary, any pertinent literary definitions that may be unfamiliar to students (see Glossary, pages 165–170).

SIGN POST:

Depending on the grade, knowledge, and skill level of the students, the teacher may not wish to include all of the suggested formats in his or her adaptation of the *Vagabond Readers* program. Select those that best suit your needs. Photocopy the age-appropriate bibliography format from the masters included with the previous lesson on the reverse of the chosen log entry formats (one is intended for younger readers and the other is for older readers). Use it with each of the new formats you select.

NOVEL SUMMARY ASSESSMENT GUIDELINES

1. **Story Gift Shop** (souvenirs taken from the story)

   Resource:
   - Story Gift Shop

   *Requirement:
   - at least fourteen points expressed in note form

   Procedure:

   The student provides information on
   - the names of two characters,
   - a personality trait and physical feature for each character,
   - the problem or conflict facing the characters,
   - the setting, including the time and the place,
   - two features of the setting using descriptive words,
   - the theme—central meaning of the story, and
   - two ways that the story affected the student's emotions. These should be more specific as the age of the reader increases.

2. **News Flash!**

   Resource:
   - News Item

   *Requirement:
   - at least seven points expressed as six complete sentences plus a headline

   Procedure:

   The student provides information about a newsworthy event in his or her novel including
   - a headline to draw the reader's attention,
   - where the event took place,
   - when it happened,
   - who it happened to,
   - what happened,
   - how it happened, and
   - why it happened.

* If there is insufficient room for all the required information on the card, students may continue the log entry on a sheet of paper and attach it to the card.

STORY GIFT SHOP

Requirement: 14 points in note form

Name _____   Class _____

Title _____   Author _____

Take souvenirs from the story including: two characters' names, personality traits, and physical features; descriptions of the conflict and the setting using descriptive words; a statement of the theme, and two ways the story affected your emotions.

_____

_____

_____

_____

_____

_____

_____

_____

_____

_____

_____

_____

NEWS FLASH!

Requirement: 6 sentences plus headline

Name _____   Class _____

Title _____   Author _____

Select and describe a newsworthy event in your book. Write your description as a news article and add a headline. Answer: **Where? When? Who? What? How? Why?**

Headline: _____

_____

_____

_____

_____

_____

_____

_____

_____

_____

NOVEL SUMMARY ASSESSMENT GUIDELINES

3. Plot Time Line

Resource:
- Time Line

*Requirement:
- at least seven points in complete sentences

Procedure:

Students list in proper sequence seven main events from the novel he or she has read including
- exposition,
- initiating incident,
- two complications,
- climax, and
- resolution (including denouement).

4. Plot Outline

Resource:
- Outline

*Requirement:
- at least fourteen points in note form

Procedure:

Students provide information on
- the four main events in the plot of the story,
- at least three minor details concerning each of those events

* If there is insufficient room for all the required information on the card, students may continue the log entry on a sheet of paper and attach it to the card.

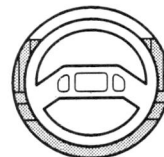

PLOT TIME LINE

Requirement: 7 complete sentences

Name: _____ Class: _____

Title: _____ Author: _____

List seven main events of the story in proper sequence, including: two items from the exposition, initiating incident, two complications, climax, and resolution.

1. _____

2. _____

3. _____

4. _____

5. _____

6. _____

7. _____

PLOT OUTLINE

Requirement: 14 points in note form

Name: _____ Class: _____

Title: _____ Author: _____

List four main events in your novel and three details for each main event.

I. _____
   A. _____
   B. _____
   C. _____

III. _____
   A. _____
   B. _____
   C. _____

II. _____
   A. _____
   B. _____
   C. _____

IV. _____
   A. _____
   B. _____
   C. _____

NOVEL SUMMARY ASSESSMENT GUIDELINES

5.   Friendly Letter

Resource:
- Friendly Letter

*Requirement:
- one paragraph containing at least seven points in complete sentences

Procedure:

The student assumes the identity of a character in the novel and writes a short friendly letter to another character.

The letter may reveal
- the relationship between the characters,
- how either character is affected by the conflict,
- how either is involved in the plot,
- the feelings and/or attitudes of either character, and
- the goals and/or motivations of either character.

6.   Plot Diagram

Resource:
- Plot Diagram

*Requirement:
- at least seven points in complete sentences

Procedure:

The student describes
- an incident that provides exposition,
- the initiating incident,
- two incidents that provide complication,
- the climax,
- the resolution, and
- the denouement.

* If there is insufficient room for all the required information on the card, then students may continue the log entry on a sheet of paper and attach it to the card.

FRIENDLY LETTER

Requirement: 7 complete sentences

Name: _____ Class: _____

Title: _____ Author: _____

Consider the relationships among the characters, their involvement in the plot and the conflict, and their feelings, attitudes, goals, and motivations. Put yourself in the place of the character writing the letter.

Dear _____ (character's name)

_____
_____
_____
_____
_____
_____
_____
_____
_____

Yours sincerely, _____

(character's name)

PLOT DIAGRAM

Requirement: 7 points in sentences

Name: _____ Class: _____

Title: _____ Author: _____

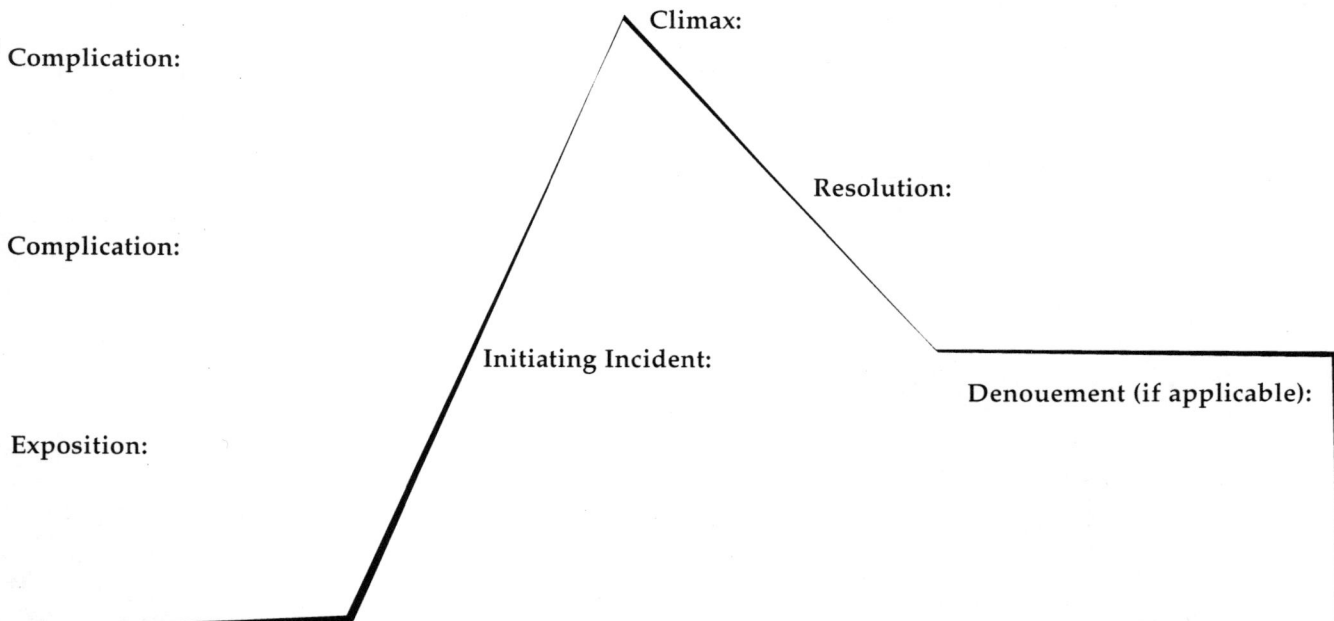

Complication:

Climax:

Complication:

Resolution:

Initiating Incident:

Exposition:

Denouement (if applicable):

NOVEL SUMMARY ASSESSMENT GUIDELINES

7. **Journal Entry**

   Resource:
   • Journal or Diary Entry

   *Requirement:
   • at least seven points in complete sentences

   Procedure:
   Assuming the identity of a character in the novel, the student writes a journal entry
   • stating what the character might believe about the theme or central meaning of the story.
   • "getting inside" the character's mind to see things from that character's point of view.

8. **Critique: Banners and Boners**

   Resource:
   • Critique

   *Requirement:
   • at least seven points in complete sentences

   Procedure:
   The student also writes
   • a sentence summarizing the book's plot,
   • three sentences telling what he or she liked about the book, and
   • three sentences telling what he or she disliked about the book.

* If there is insufficient room for all the required information on the card, students may continue the log entry on a sheet of paper and attach it to the card.

JOURNAL ENTRY

Requirement: 7 complete sentences

Name: _____ Class: _____

Title: _____ Author: _____

Express what the main character might believe about the story's theme or central meaning.

Dear Diary,

_____
_____
_____
_____
_____
_____
_____
_____
_____

Signed _____
character's name

CRITIQUE: Banners & Boners

Requirement: 7 complete sentences

Name: _____ Class: _____

Title: _____ Author: _____

This book was about _____
_____

What I Liked About the Book

1. _____
_____
2. _____
_____
3. _____
_____

What I Disliked About the Book

1. _____
_____
2. _____
_____
3. _____
_____

Chapter Three: Launching into Literature

FANTASY

BIOGRAPHY

FOLKLORE

AUTOBIOGRAPHY

HISTORICAL FICTION

SCIENCE FICTION

Getting Perspective

Heather: I've noticed that as many students choose books they tend to choose series books or those by a certain author. How can we motivate them to broaden their reading experiences?

Kori: Why don't we introduce the major genres of literature as travel companies, each with its own unique approach to serving clients. After all, even vagabonds can enjoy the convenience of a well-planned tour now and then!

Heather: Great idea! As they learn more about the various literary forms, they may be inclined to take a "road less traveled."

Kori: Maybe then they will eventually realize that for both travelers and readers, freedom of choice involves more than just the right to choose a goal or destination.

Heather: Right! It means gaining the knowledge and skills to make the best choice.

Kori: As the students participate in the activities offered by the travel companies, they will begin to realize just how vast the universe really is.

Heather: They will also be better prepared for the journeys they plan on their own.

Kori: And they will discover that they gain more freedom rather than less. And isn't that what being a vagabond is all about?

Types of Transportation—Fiction vs. Nonfiction

Many upper elementary and junior high school students find it difficult to differentiate between fiction and nonfiction. This lesson helps them to differentiate between the two.

SPECIFIC LEARNER EXPECTATIONS:

- Students begin to distinguish between fiction and nonfiction.

RESOURCES:

- several examples of fiction
- several examples of nonfiction, including biography
- Overhead Projection "What Fiction Books Do for Writers and Readers"

TEACHER:

- uses Overhead Projection "What Fiction Books Do for Writers and Readers" to lead a discussion on what fiction books do for the writer and what they do for the reader.
- gives a brief description of sample books.
- allows students time to peruse the sample books.

TEACHER AND STUDENTS:

- sort books into two distinct categories—fiction and nonfiction.
- discuss difference between fiction and nonfiction.

STUDENTS:

- in groups of three or four create acronyms* for "fiction" and "nonfiction" or another mnemonic device to help them remember the difference between the two.
- display or share acronyms or mnemonic devices with the class.

SIGN POST:

Use acronyms sparingly. If the students have too many they will not be able to remember them.

What Fiction Books Do
for Writers and Readers

For the Writer

Fiction allows writers to rethink and retell their experiences in order to understand them better.

For the Reader

Fiction inspires the readers' feelings and imagination. It provides entertainment, enjoyment, and a greater knowledge of human experience.

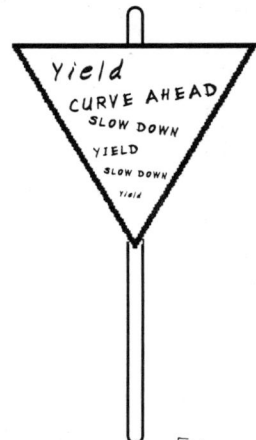

Identifying Travel Companies—Genres

This lesson introduces students to literary terms and six major genres of literature. Students see how these genres are related and learn to distinguish between them.

SPECIFIC LEARNER EXPECTATIONS:
- Students are introduced to the major literary genres.
- Students gain experience in classifying literature.

RESOURCES:
- several sample books of each of the following genres: modern realistic, historical, science fiction, fantasy, folklore, and biography
- Student Reference "Tracking Guide"
- Student Performance Master "Travel Directory"

TEACHER:
- leads a discussion on the meanings of fiction, nonfiction, novel, genre, and literature. (See Glossary on pages 165–170.)
- gives a brief summary of the content of each sample novel in random order. Back cover summaries may serve this purpose.

    OR

- reads a short excerpt from each of the novels.
- allows students time to peruse the books, paying attention to the cover, the chapter titles, any illustrations, and the summary on the book jacket.
- leads students in a discussion of ways to classify or categorize the novels.
- uses a sample novel to demonstrate the use of the "Tracking Guide".

TEACHER AND STUDENTS:

- compare suggested definitions to those given on the Student Performance Master "Travel Directory."
- compare suggested ways of classifying novels with the six genres given on the Student Reference "Tracking Guide."
- check several dictionaries for the definition of literature and generate a class definition.

STUDENTS:

- write the class definition of literature in the space provided on the Student Performance Master "Travel Directory".
- individually or in groups of three or four
    1. use the Student Reference "Tracking Guide" to classify six different novels.
    2. record the titles of these six novels in the appropriate example spaces provided on the Student Performance Master "Travel Directory." Students will complete the characteristics section of the "Travel Directory" as they learn about each genre in subsequent lessons.
- keep the "Tracking Guide" and "Travel Directory" for future reference.

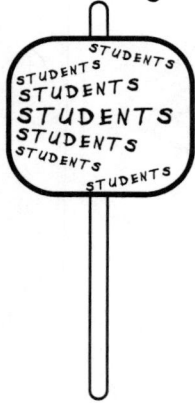

TRACKING GUIDE

The chart below will help you to classify a book as fiction or nonfiction and also, in the case of a novel, to determine its genre. Keep this guide for future reference.

Directions: Beginning at "Start," decide which of the two statements best describes the book. Follow the appropriate arrows until you arrive at a classification.

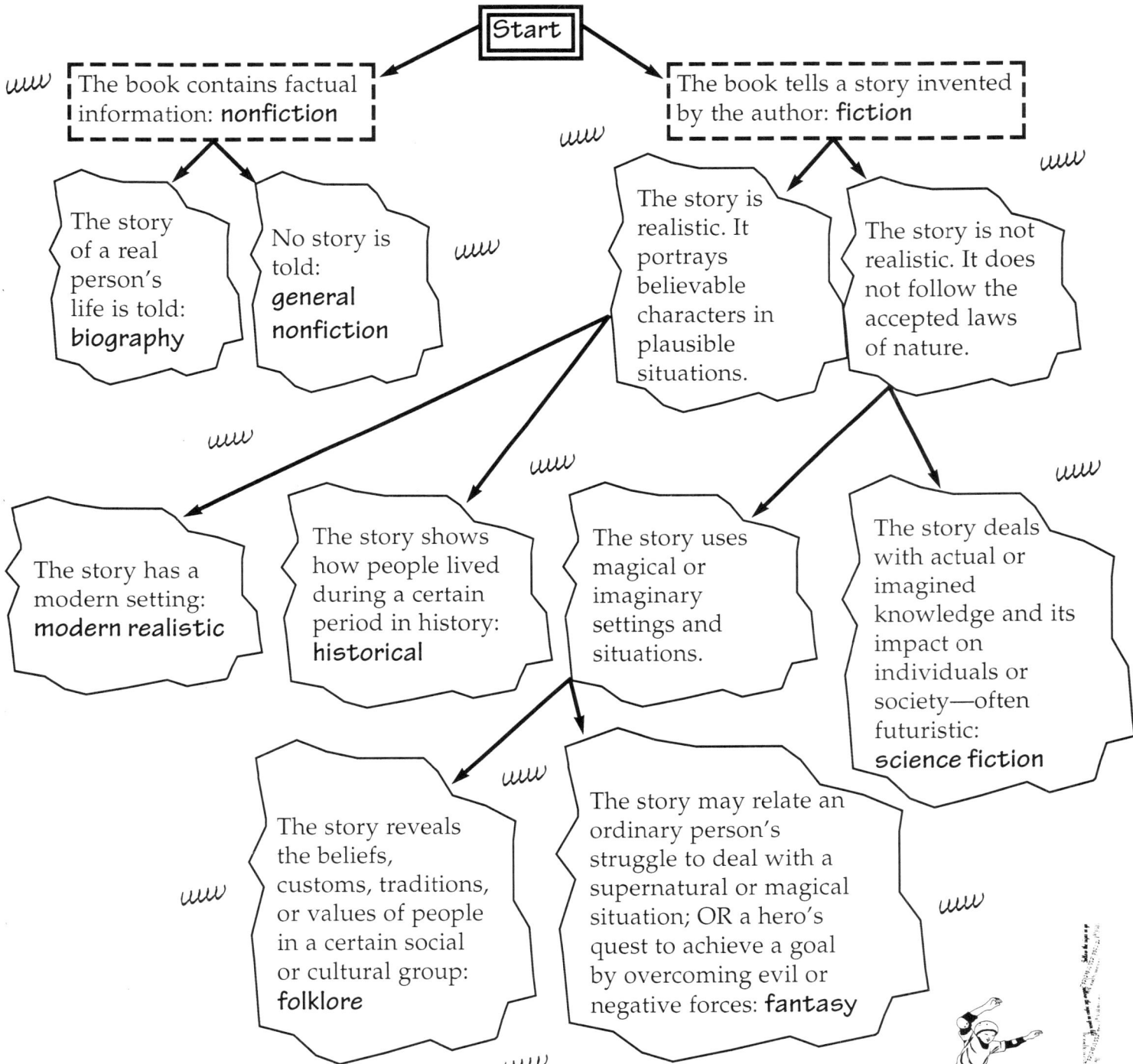

Start

The book contains factual information: **nonfiction**

The book tells a story invented by the author: **fiction**

The story of a real person's life is told: **biography**

No story is told: **general nonfiction**

The story is realistic. It portrays believable characters in plausible situations.

The story is not realistic. It does not follow the accepted laws of nature.

The story has a modern setting: **modern realistic**

The story shows how people lived during a certain period in history: **historical**

The story uses magical or imaginary settings and situations.

The story deals with actual or imagined knowledge and its impact on individuals or society—often futuristic: **science fiction**

The story reveals the beliefs, customs, traditions, or values of people in a certain social or cultural group: **folklore**

The story may relate an ordinary person's struggle to deal with a supernatural or magical situation; OR a hero's quest to achieve a goal by overcoming evil or negative forces: **fantasy**

Vagabond Readers
©1997 F.P. Hendriks Publishing Ltd.
Permission to reproduce

TRAVEL DIRECTORY

As well as defining literary terms, this directory indicates the travel mode that you as a "vagabond reader" can associate with a particular literary genre. Keep this directory for future reference.

Definitions:

Fiction: a literary work that is a product of a writer's imagination. It may or may not be based on fact.

Nonfiction: a literary work providing factual information about a subject or topic.

Novel: a fictional work of considerable length having a plot that is revealed by the actions, speech, and thoughts of the characters.

Genre: a distinct class or category of literary work characterized by a particular form.

Literature: _____

_____

Genres:

1. **Historical**—*Hustler's Stagecoach*

Characteristics:

_____

_____

Examples:

_____

_____

_____

_____

Travel Directory (continued)

2.   **Modern Realistic**—*Mega-rapid Air and Rail*

Characteristics:

_____

_____

_____

Examples:

_____

_____

_____

3.   **Fantasy**—*Fringe's Magic Carpets*

Characteristics:

_____

_____

_____

Examples:

_____

_____

_____

Travel Directory (continued)

4. **Science Fiction**—*Space Flyer Intergalactic Express*

Characteristics:

_____

_____

_____

Examples:

_____

_____

_____

5. **Biography and Autobiography**—*Briney's Shipping*

Characteristics:

_____

_____

_____

Examples:

_____

_____

_____

Travel Directory (continued)

6.   **Folklore**—*Feather Landing Winged Chariots*
      This is a general class that includes songs, sayings, and dances, as well as the following types of literature:

a) Legend:	a popular story handed down from earlier times; seen as historical although it cannot be verified
b) Folktale:	a traditional story that is anonymous, timeless, and placeless, handed down (often orally) by the common people of a country or region from one generation to the next
c) Fable:	a brief tale or story that teaches a useful lesson or has a moral, often using animal characters that speak and act like human beings
d) Myth:	a traditional story that uses supernatural beings and events to explain a cultural belief, a practice, or a natural phenomenon

Characteristics:

_____

_____

_____

Examples:

_____

_____

_____

Vagabond Readers
©1997 F.P. Hendriks Publishing Ltd.
Permission to reproduce

Historical and Modern Realistic Fiction

In order for students to differentiate among the various literary genres they need a frame of reference. This lesson provides a reference for modern realistic and historical literature.

SPECIFIC LEARNER EXPECTATIONS:

- Students are introduced to the characteristics of historical and modern realistic novels and practice identifying examples.
- Students practice revising a passage from a historical novel into modern realistic form and vice versa, to understand the difference between the genres.

RESOURCES:

- Overhead Projection "Company Characteristics, Part 1"
- from the previous lesson, Student Performance Master "Travel Directory" (pages 88–91)
- large chart paper

TEACHER:

- displays characteristics of modern realistic literature using Overhead Projection "Company Characteristics, Part 1."
- displays characteristics of historical literature.
- gives directions for student activity.

STUDENTS:

- enter the characteristics of historical and modern realistic literature on Student Performance Master "Travel Directory" as they are displayed.
- choose two examples of novels from each genre and use these to complete the examples section on the Student Performance Master "Travel Directory."
- carry out activity on the next page in pairs.

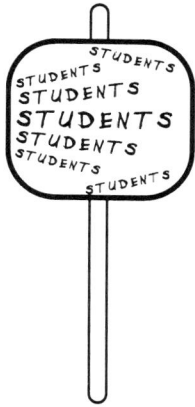

Students, continued:

- in pairs:
    1. Student A finds an interesting passage of one or two paragraphs from a historical novel.
    2. Student B finds an interesting passage of one or two paragraphs from a modern realistic novel.
    3. Students A and B record their passages on chart paper and read them to each other.
    4. Students A and B rewrite each other's selections in the opposite genre, changing modern realistic to historical, and historical to modern realistic.
    5. Student pairs read the rewritten passages to each other.

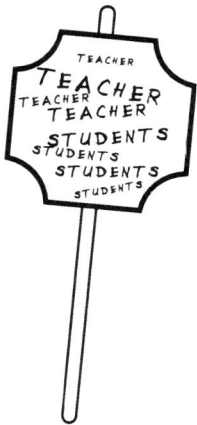

TEACHER AND STUDENTS:

- carry out a carousel activity by
    1. posting the original and rewritten selections around the room and
    2. moving in pairs from one selection to the next, noting the rewriting necessary to change a story from one genre to another.
- discuss the strategies used by students to rewrite the passages. This "thinking about thinking" activity, called metacognition, is a way of helping students to think about how they solve problems or challenges so that in a similar situation they can use some of those same strategies.
- note these strategies on chart paper and post them for a time in the classroom.

Company Characteristics, Part 1

1. Historical (Hustler's Stagecoach)
    - reflects a specific period of history
    - gives an accurate description of how people lived at that time
    - set approximately fifty or more years in the past

2. Modern Realistic (Mega-rapid Air and Rail)
    - deals with serious problems and situations
    - gives an accurate description of how people live
    - has a modern setting

3. Fantasy (Fringe's Magic Carpets)
    - involves imaginary settings and situations
    - goes beyond accepted laws of nature
    - exaggerates characters and events
    - deals with the supernatural or the magical

4. Science Fiction (Space Flyer Intergalactic Express)
    - describes adventures in outer space, on other planets, or in the future
    - based on knowledge of science and technology
    - often set in the future

Company Characteristics, Part 2

5.   Biography and Autobiography (Briney's Shipping)

Autobiographies are biographies written by people about themselves and are included in the general classification of biography.

- based on a person's life
- presents accurate information and is therefore considered nonfiction
- tells about a person in the setting in which he or she lived or is living

6.   Folklore (Feather Landing Winged Chariots)

- passed down from generation to generation
- reveals the beliefs, customs, traditions, or values of ordinary people in various social and cultural groups
- often incorporates adventure and magic

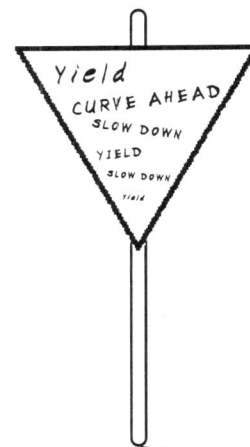

HUSTLER'S TOURS

Historical Literature for Younger Readers

Avi. *The True Confessions of Charlotte Doyle*. New York: Avon, 1990.
> Charlotte discovers her transatlantic voyage will be anything but peaceful.

Drucker, Malka and Michael Halperin. *Jacob's Rescue: A Holocaust Story*. New York: Dell, 1993.
> Eight-year-old Jacob is hidden from the Nazis by the Roslan family.

Gray, Elizabeth Jane. *Adam of the Road*. Markham, ON: Penguin, 1942.
> Adam travels the open roads of thirteenth century England searching for his missing father and a red spaniel named Nick.

MacLachlan, Patricia. *Sarah, Plain and Tall*. Toronto, ON: Fitzhenry & Whiteside, 1985.
> A tall, plain woman comes to stay with a motherless prairie family.

Smucker, Barbara. *Underground to Canada*. Toronto, ON: Penguin, 1977.
> When workers from the "underground railway" offer to help Julilly and her friend Liza reach Canada, the girls are ready.

Historical Literature for Older Readers

Bellingham, Brenda. *Storm Child*. Toronto, ON: James Lorimer, 1985.
> Isobel's Peigan grandparents help her understand who she is.

Cushman, Karen. *The Midwife's Apprentice*. New York: HarperCollins, 1995.
> A homeless girl begins a new life as a midwife's apprentice during the MIddle Ages.

Fleischman, Paul. *The Borning Room*. New York: HarperCollins, 1991.
> Dying in the same room where she was born in 1851, Georgina recalls the highlights of her life on the Ohio frontier.

Pearson, Kit. *Looking at the Moon*. Toronto, ON: Penguin, 1991.
> Norah learns about growing up while living with her wealthy grandmother in Toronto during World War II.

Taylor, Cora. *Summer of the Mad Monk*. Toronto, ON: Douglas & McIntyre, 1994.
> A mysterious stranger changes the life of a young boy during the Great Depression.

MEGA-RAPID TOURS

Modern Realistic Literature for Younger Readers

Andrews, Jan. *Keri*. Toronto, ON: Douglas & McIntyre, 1996.
>   Keri is determined to save a beached humpback whale, no matter how impossible the odds.

Blume, Judy. *Here's to You, Rachel Robinson*. New York: Dell, 1993.
>   A straight-A student discovers that real life is much more interesting than "perfect life."

Dankas, John. *Hockey Night in Transcona*. Toronto, ON: James Lorimer, 1995.
>   Cody's skill at hockey earns him a spot on the community team, but it's the same spot that Stu, the coach's son, loses.

Naylor, Phyllis Reynolds. *Shiloh*. New York: Bantam Doubleday Dell, 1991.
>   Marty tries to figure out a way to get a young beagle away from its cruel master.

Paterson, Katherine. *Bridge to Terabithia*. New York: Harper & Row, 1977.
>   A Virginia boy and the girl who befriends him share a secret hideaway.

Modern Realistic Literature for Older Readers

Halvorson, Marilyn. *Stranger on the Run*. Toronto, ON: Stoddard, 1992.
>   After a young native man offers him refuge on a cattle ranch, Steve learns about new kinds of survival.

Morck, Irene. *Between Brothers*. Toronto, ON: Stoddard, 1992.
>   The precarious relationship between two brothers is tested when they fall for the same girl.

Reynolds, Marilyn. *Detour for Emmy*. Buena Park, CA: Morning Glory Press, 1993.
>   Emmy matures while facing the consequences of her teenage pregnancy.

Spalding, Andrea. *Finders Keepers*. Victoria, BC: Orca, 1995.
>   As he uncovers clues about the origins of the lance head he found in a field, Danny gains valuable insights about himself, including new ways of handling his problems at school.

Trembath, Don. *The Tuesday Cafe*. Victoria, BC: Orca, 1996.
>   When a juvenile court judge orders Harper to write an essay on how he is going to turn his life around, Harper's mother enrolls him in a writing class.

Fantasy and Science Fiction Literature

In order for students to differentiate among the various literary genres they need a frame of reference. This lesson provides a reference for fantasy and science fiction.

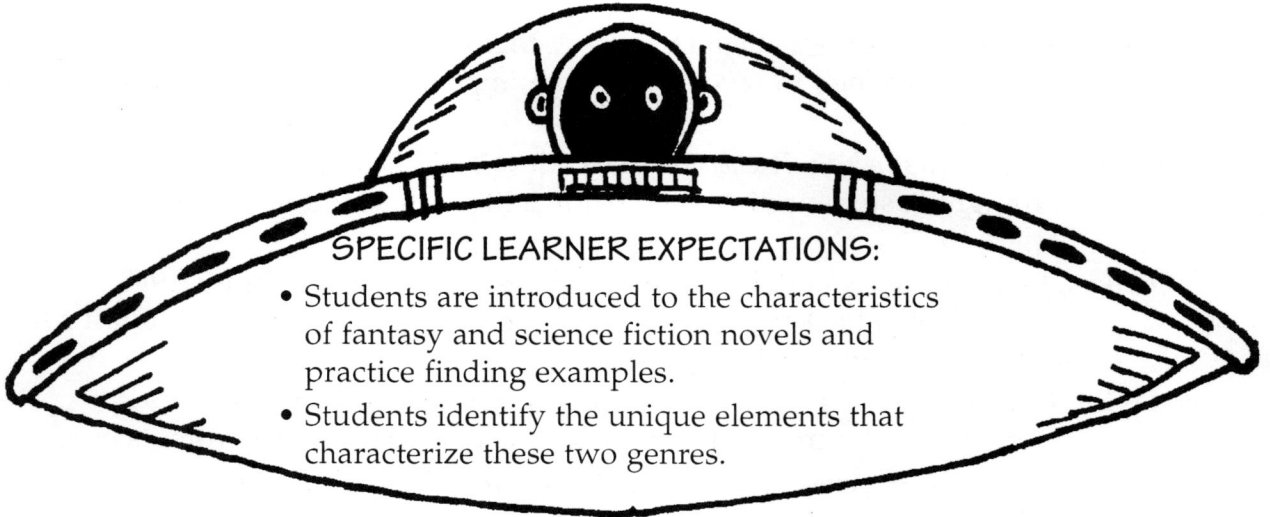

SPECIFIC LEARNER EXPECTATIONS:

- Students are introduced to the characteristics of fantasy and science fiction novels and practice finding examples.
- Students identify the unique elements that characterize these two genres.

RESOURCES:

- from the previous lesson, Overhead Projection "Company Characteristics, Part 1" (page 94)
- from a previous lesson, Student Performance Master "Travel Directory" (pages 88–91)
- Student Performance Master "Come Fly with Me"

TEACHER:

- presents characteristics of fantasy using Overhead Projection "Company Characteristics, Part 1."
- presents characteristics of science fiction.
- gives directions for the student activity.

STUDENTS:

- enter the characteristics of fantasy and science fiction on Student Performance Master "Travel Directory" as displayed.
- choose two examples of novels from each genre and use these to complete the examples section on the Student Performance Master "Travel Directory."
- carry out the activity on the next page in pairs.

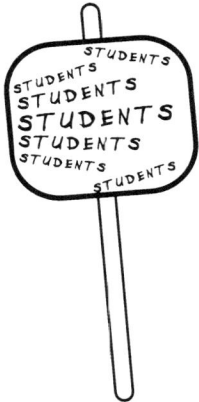

Students, continued:

- in pairs:

    1. Student A chooses a fantasy and browses through it, selecting examples of characters, settings, and events that indicate the work is a fantasy and entering these on the Student Performance Master "Come Fly with Me."

    2. Student B chooses a science fiction novel and selects elements that show the work is science fiction and enters these on the lines provided.

    3. Students compare their selections.

TEACHER AND STUDENTS:

- use the completed Student Performance Masters "Come Fly with Me" to discuss the differences and similarities between science fiction and fantasy.

ALTERNATE ROUTE:

This can also be a more game-like activity. Once students have chosen selections, have pairs collect into two teams. Each student reads his or her chosen passage to the other team who must decide which genre the story belongs to. Points are awarded for correct answers.

This activity can also be used as a review and expanded to include those excerpts taken from the modern realistic and historical novels of the previous lesson.

COME FLY WITH ME

Directions: Indicate at the top of the chart whether your book is fantasy or science fiction. Select characters, settings, and events that reveal the novel's genre and enter them on the chart beneath the appropriate heading.

Example:

My novel is an example of _____ **fantasy** _____ .

Characters	Setting	Events
unicorn	lilac wood	An old woman puts a spell on a unicorn

My novel is an example of   .

_____

Characters	Setting	Events

FRINGE'S MAGIC CARPETS

Fantasy Literature for Younger Readers

Avi. *Bright Shadow*. New York: MacMillan, 1985.
  Morwenna has five wishes to make on behalf of her country's citizens.
Babbitt, Natalie. *Tuck Everlasting*. Toronto, ON: Collins, 1975.
  The Tuck family's magical spring is the source of their eternal youth.
Charnas, Suzy McKee. *The Bronze King*. Toronto, ON: Bantam, 1985.
  With only a street fiddler and his young friend to help her, Tina takes on a creature of the darkness.
Jones, Terry. *Nicobobinus*. Markham, ON: Penguin, 1985.
  Nicobobinus and his friend Rosie encounter many difficulties as they search for the Land of the Dragons.
Kaye, M.M. *The Ordinary Princess*. New York: Simon & Schuster, 1986.
  Princess Amy is so ordinary, no prince can be found to marry her, but that doesn't bother Amy.

Fantasy Literature for Older Readers

Bates, Martine. *The Dragon's Tapestry*. Red Deer, AB: Red Deer College Press, 1992.
  Marwen's search for a dragon leads her to lost lands and powerful magic.
Beagle, Peter S. *The Last Unicorn*. Toronto, ON: Random House, 1992.
  An immortal, exquisitely beautiful unicorn searches for her lost fellows.
Lackey, Mercedes. *Arrows of the Queen*. New York: Donald Wollheim, 1987.
  Talia must master the awakening powers of her mind in order to help the other Heralds protect the queen.
Meyers, Walter Dean. *The Legend of Tarik*. Toronto, ON: Scholastic, 1981.
  Young Tarik sets out to avenge the slaughter of his family by an evil tyrant.
Murphy, Shirley Rousseau. *The Ivory Lyre*. Toronto, ON: Fitzhenry & Whiteside, 1987.
  Only the union of human spirit and dragon magic can restore the memory of freedom to the inhabitants of Tirror.

SPACE FLYER TOURS

Science Fiction Literature for Younger Readers

Coville, Bruce. *Aliens Ate My Homework*. New York: Pocket Books, 1993.
   A tiny spaceship causes trouble for Rod.

Klause, Annette Curtis. *Alien Secrets*. New York: Bantam Doubleday Dell, 1993.
   After being expelled from a boarding school in space, Puck tries to help a fellow
   traveler named Hush find a stolen treasure.

L'Engle, Madeleine. *A Wrinkle in Time*. New York: Bantam, 1976.
   Meg and her family receive a visit from a stranger from another dimension.

Pinkwater, Daniel Manus. *Lizard Music*. New York: Bantam, 1976.
   Intelligent lizards tell a young boy of an invasion from outer space.

Yep, Lawrence. *Sweetheart*. Toronto, ON: Fitzhenry & Whiteside, 1973.
   A songmaster's gift kindles, in Tyree's people, fears that tear their community apart.

Science Fiction Literature for Older Readers

Crichton, Michael. *Jurassic Park*. New York: Ballantine, 1991.
   Dinosaur DNA is cloned with disastrous results.

Farmer, Nancy. *The Ear, the Eye, and the Arm*. New York: Penguin, 1994.
   After three children from Zimbabwe are kidnapped and put to work in a twenty-first
   century plastic mine, mutant detectives use special powers to search for them.

Godfrey, Martyn. *Alien Wargames*. Toronto, ON: Scholastic, 1984.
   With the arrival of humans, Darsa faces a crisis in which she must choose between
   her own code of honor and the safety of her people.

Hughes, Monica. *The Tomorrow City*. London: Mammoth, 1978.
   Disaster threatens the citizens of Thompsonville as a computer uses increasingly
   ruthless means to control their lives.

Sleator, William. *The Duplicate*. Toronto, ON: Bantam, 1988.
   David creates a clone who turns against him.

Folklore and Biographical Literature

In order for students to differentiate among the various literary genres they need a frame of reference. This lesson provides a reference for biography and folklore.

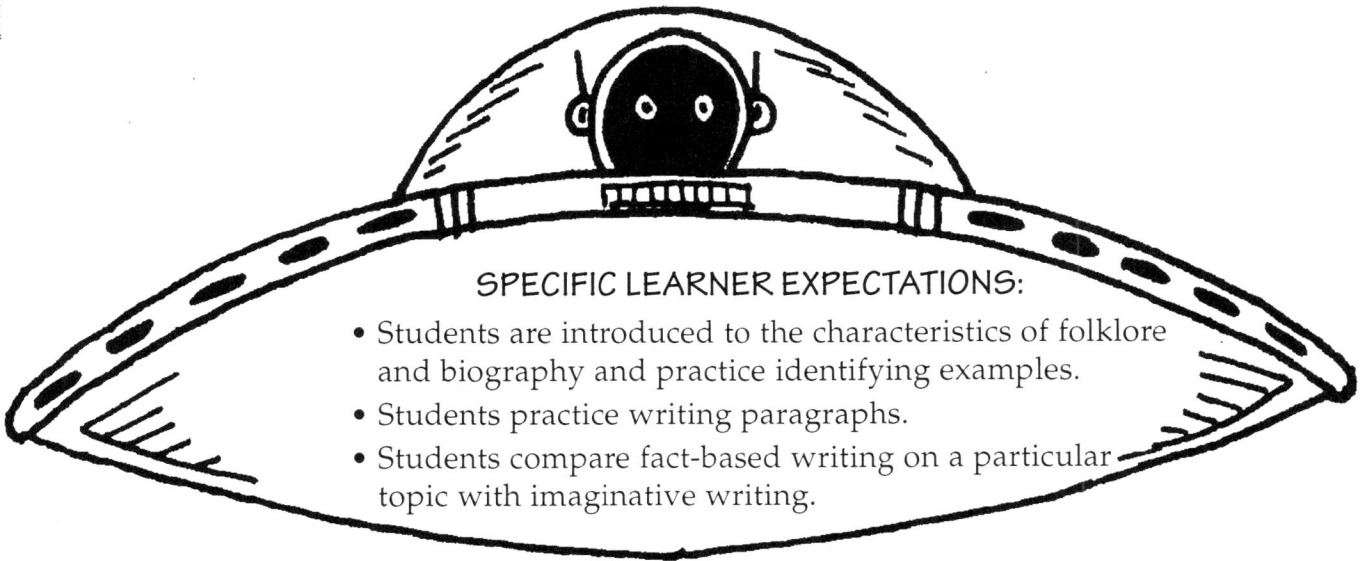

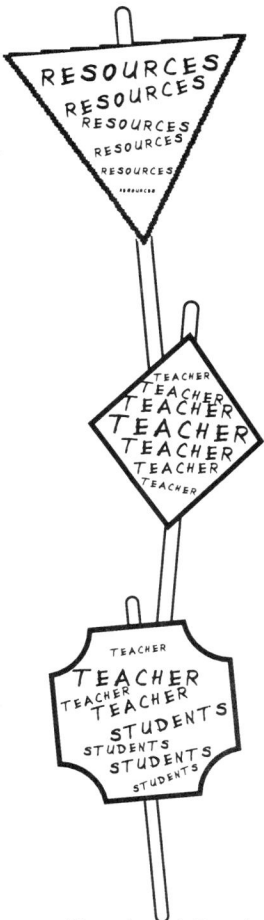

SPECIFIC LEARNER EXPECTATIONS:

- Students are introduced to the characteristics of folklore and biography and practice identifying examples.
- Students practice writing paragraphs.
- Students compare fact-based writing on a particular topic with imaginative writing.

RESOURCES:

- from a previous lesson, Overhead Projection "Company Characteristics, Part 2" (page 95)
- from a previous lesson, Student Performance Master "Travel Directory" (pages 88–91)
- Student Performance Master "Bio Transport"
- Student Performance Master "Ferrying Folklore"

TEACHER:

- presents characteristics of folklore using Overhead Projection "Company Characteristics, Part 2."
- presents characteristics of biography.
- gives directions for student activity.

TEACHER AND STUDENTS:

- brainstorm natural events, bodies, or phenomena, e.g. tornado, volcanic eruption, lightning, earthquake, comet, northern lights, tidal wave and so on.

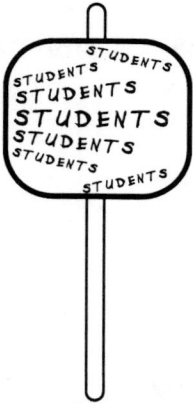

STUDENTS:

- enter the characteristics of folklore and biography on the Student Performance Master "Travel Directory" as they are displayed.
- choose two examples of books from each genre and use these to complete the examples section on the Student Performance Master "Travel Directory."
- in groups of four:
    1. choose a natural wonder from the brainstormed list.
    2. two students complete Student Performance Master "Bio Transport," explaining the natural wonder scientifically using a biographical format.
    3. two other students complete Student Performance Master "Ferrying Folklore," explaining the same event or phenomenon imaginatively.
    4. share and compare their explanations between the pairs.
    5. share and compare their explanations among the groups of four.

Problems?

Travel Insurance

Refer to Travel Insurance in Chapter 1, pages 11–12.

BIO TRANSPORT

Directions: Complete the following using an encyclopedia with information about the natural wonder you chose.

1. State where, when, and under what conditions the natural wonder is most likely to be found.

   _____

   _____

   _____

2. Explain, in steps, what is known about the wonder's formation or occurrence.

   _____

   _____

   _____

   _____

   _____

3. List any identifying characteristics of the natural wonder.

   _____

   _____

   _____

4. Invent a name for the natural wonder. _____

5. Using the information above, write a one-paragraph biography or life history of the natural wonder. Be sure to personalize your bio by referring to the natural wonder by the name you invented. Use the back of this sheet for your finished biography.

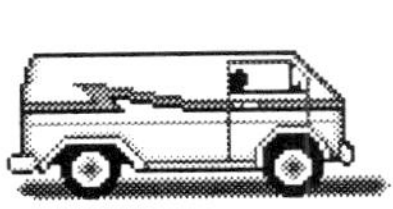

STUDENT PERFORMANCE MASTER

NAME _____

FERRYING FOLKLORE

Directions: Complete the following about the natural wonder you chose using your imagination.

1. List qualities that you think the natural wonder would have if it existed as a person or an animal.

_____

_____

_____

2. Wind, thunder, and rain are associated with the phenomenon of lightning. What other aspects of nature are associated with the natural wonder you chose or were assigned?

_____

_____

3. Invent names for the natural wonder and each of the forces associated with it.

_____

_____

4. Think of a situation involving the associated forces (secondary characters) that results in the appearance of the natural wonder (main character). Write this as a one-sentence plot summary.

_____

_____

_____

5. Combine your answers to the previous questions in a one-paragraph fictional explanation for the existence of the natural wonder you chose. Be sure to refer to your characters by the names you invented. Use the back of this sheet for your finished product.

FEATHER LANDING TOURS

Folklore for Younger Readers

Croll, Carolyn. *The Little Snowgirl*. New York: Putnam & Grosset, 1989.
    A Russian couple's wish for a child is fulfilled when the snowgirl in the yard comes alive.

Esbensen, Barbara Juster. *Ladder to the Sky*. Toronto, ON: Little & Brown, 1989.
    After sickness and death are sent down by the Great Spirit, the Ojibwa people must learn how to heal themselves with flowers and herbs.

Kurtz, Jane. *Fire on the Mountain*. Toronto, ON: Simon & Shuster, 1994.
    A shepherd boy and his sister must outfox their rich master at his own game.

Mollel, Tololwa M. *The Orphan Boy*. Toronto, ON: Oxford University Press, 1990.
    The old man who adopts Kileken becomes desperate to know the secret of the orphan boy's strange powers.

Rhoads, Dorothy. *The Corn Grows Ripe*. Toronto, ON: Penguin, 1956.
    When his father is badly injured, Tigre must plant the corn his Mayan family needs to survive.

Folklore for Older Readers

Irving, Washington. *The Legend of Sleepy Hollow*. Aerie Books, 1987.
    Schoolteacher Ichabod Crane is fascinated by tales of a shadowy soldier who rides headless through the night.

Pyle, Howard. *The Merry Adventures of Robin Hood*. New York: Baronet Books, 1987.
    Robin and his band strive to protect the people of Nottingham from the greedy barons who control the countryside.

Steinbeck, John. *The Pearl*. Toronto, ON: Bantam, 1986.
    A giant pearl brings disaster to a simple man and his family.

Stevenson, Robert Louis. *Dr. Jekyll and Mr. Hyde*. Toronto, ON: Bantam, 1886.
    Dr. Jekyll's friends are mystified by his relationship with the wicked Mr. Hyde.

White, T.H. *The Sword in the Stone*. London: HarperCollins, 1938.
    After Merlyn the magician becomes his tutor, an adopted orphan learns about the important things in life.

BRINEY'S TOURS

Biography for Younger Readers

Adler, David. *A Picture Book of Anne Frank.* New York: Holiday House, 1993.
Adler describes Anne's life as she and her family hid from the Nazis in an Amsterdam attic.

Davidson, Margaret. *Helen Keller's Teacher.* Toronto, ON: Scholastic, 1965.
Davidson describes Annie Sullivan's struggle to free Helen from a dark, silent prison.

Fritz, Jean. *Homesick: My Own Story.* New York: Dell, 1982.
Jean Fritz relates her own life from her birth in China to the present.

Gleiter, Jan and Kathleen Thompson. *Pocahontas.* Toronto, ON: Raintree, 1985.
A Powhatan Indian woman helps maintain the peace between her people and the English colonists at Jamestown, Virginia.

Huynh, Quang Nhuong. *The Land I Lost.* Toronto, ON: Fitzhenry & Whiteside, 1982.
Huynh explains what it was like to grow up on the central highlands Vietnam.

Biography for Older Readers

Burch, Jennings Michael. *They Cage the Animals at Night.* New York: New American Library, 1984.
Burch tells of a lost childhood and a little boy who finally found the courage to reach out for love.

Duncan, Lois. *Who Killed My Daughter?* New York: Bantam Doubleday Dell, 1992.
Lois Duncan documents her own search for her daughter's killer.

Higa, Tomiko. *Girl with the White Flag.* New York, Dell, 1992.
Higa records her childhood ordeal of wartime survival in Okinawa.

White, Ryan and Ann Marie Cunningham. *Ryan White: My Own Story.* New York: Penguin, 1991.
This book explains how Ryan contracted AIDS and how he became a spokesman for issues concerning the disease prior to his death.

Zindel, Paul. *The Pigman and Me.* Toronto, ON: Bantam, 1991.
Zindel explains how his teenage years were enriched by a unique mentor.

A Light in the "Dark Room"

Heather: Whew! Our vagabond readers are off and running… or flying… or voyaging!

Kori: The wall chart in the library is filling up with stickers. The students are progressing toward their goals. They are also learning a lot about literature and making the reading-writing connection in their log books.

Heather: I think the travelers are ready for the next step. They are beginning to see through their literary adventures how authors use words to help form pictures in the minds of their readers. Now the students need to practice making word pictures of their own.

Kori: We could start by exploring why they chose certain reading journeys over others. The surveys the students completed earlier in the year can help.

Heather: The discussion will be a good way to introduce a lesson on leads: how they capture our attention and give us a sense of what is coming later in the story.

Kori The students are meeting many interesting people as they travel.

Heather: So we will need to look closely at how authors develop their characters.

Kori: Your use of the word "develop" gave me a picture of a writer dipping his work in a bath of mysterious chemicals. Also, students need to be choosy about specific words and expressions to get across feelings and ideas.

Heather: You're right. Overusing weak words in writing is like taking photos on a foggy day. The end result for both writer and photographer is a gray, fuzzy image.

Kori: Where the photographer stands when he clicks the shutter is another factor that affects the quality of his work.

Heather: Good idea! Perhaps we should conclude this section of the program with a study of point of view.

Kori: Let's get out the photo album.

Leads

This lesson may be linked to the reading surveys students completed at the beginning of the program. Encourage the students to think again about why they choose certain books to read and reject others.

SPECIFIC LEARNER EXPECTATIONS:

- Students begin to make predictions about their reading.
- Students write interesting leads for their own stories.

RESOURCES:

- books the students are reading or have read previously
- Overhead Projections "Leads: *Freedom Crossing*"(for younger readers), "Leads: *Until Whatever*" (for older readers), or sample lead of teacher's own choice
- Student Performance Masters "Thinking About Choices" and "Latitude for Attitudes" on pages 30–33.

TEACHER:

- prepares the students to bring the books they are reading to class and to read the beginning of the book orally to give an example of a lead.
- displays sample lead and directs discussion about what makes it a good lead.
- instructs the students to take turns reading the first page of their books and then have the other students predict what the rest of the story will be about.

TEACHER AND STUDENTS:

- read sample lead.
- discuss questions such as:
    1. What helped you make predictions about the story?
    2. Do you like or dislike this lead? Why?
    3. What words or techniques does the author use to "grab" your attention?

Teacher and Students, continued:

• discuss the techniques authors use to "grab the readers attention." These may include:

1. foreshadowing,
2. flashback, and
3. using sensory descriptions to create a mood.

STUDENTS:

• in groups of three or four, take turns reading leads and making predictions about what will happen later in the story.

• write leads for an existing story from their writing folders or for a new story using one or more of the techniques used in the leads others have read aloud.

SIGN POSTS:

Students need advance notice that they must finish reading a book or review a book that they have already read before doing this lesson.

More lessons on writing leads employing techniques used by published authors can be found in *Becoming Better Writers* by Shelley Peterson.*

* Peterson, Shelley. *Becoming Better Writers*. Edmonton, AB: F.P. Hendriks, 1995.

Leads

Excerpt from *Freedom Crossing**
by Margaret Goff Clark

"Twelve–thirty! Laura Eastman had been lying awake for nearly two hours, waiting for sleep that would not come. From the oak tree outside her window she heard a screech owl's quavery call. A moment later came the mournful howling of a pack of dogs.

Laura punched her pillow despairingly. Two weeks had passed since she'd returned to the family farm near Lewiston, N.Y., and everything still seemed strange, unfamiliar. The autumn smells of dry leaves and fallen apples, the brisk, cool air of western New York State, and most of all, the hard twang of northern voices, were almost foreign to her after living for four years in the South. Even her own father seemed like a stranger, married to a new wife. And Bert, her brother, had changed most of all."

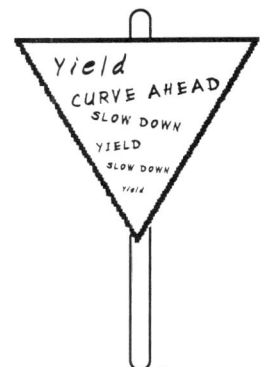

* Clark, Margaret Goff. *Freedom Crossing*. New York: Scholastic, 1980.

Vagabond Readers
©1997 F.P. Hendriks Publishing Ltd.
Permission to reproduce for display

Leads

Excerpt from *Until Whatever** by Martha Humphreys

It's Wednesday, the second day of school. I've stopped by my locker to pick up a book for first-period class. Across the hall a group of kids I usually hang around with are laughing and talking.

"Karen!" Rae Scudder breaks away from the group and darts up to me. Her face is flushed, her dark hair tousled. "Have you heard?" she gasps.

"Heard what?"

"Karen, everyone's talking about it."

I sigh. Rae has this habit of turning every bit of news, every conversation, into some big, suspenseful thing.

"At least," she goes on, "all our friends are talking about it."

And they're the ones who matter, I think. That's what would be in Rae's mind, she is a bit of a snob. "Just tell me what it is." More resigned than curious, I shut my locker.

"Connie Tibbs has AIDS."

* Humphreys, Martha. *Until Whatever*. New York: Scholastic, 1991.

Character Development, Part 1

This lesson makes students aware of various methods of characterization. It demonstrates how showing a character in action gives the reader a clearer, brighter picture of his or her personality than when direct description is used.

> ## SPECIFIC LEARNER EXPECTATIONS:
> - The students begin to identify techniques of character development in a story they are reading.

RESOURCES:

- age-appropriate Overhead Projection "Character Development, Telling vs Showing" (Excerpts from *Island of the Blue Dolphins* for younger readers or *Izzy Will-Nilly* for older readers)
    OR
- one example each of direct (telling) and indirect (showing) characterization
- Overhead Projection/Student Performance Master "To Tell or to Show?"

TEACHER:

- uses the examples of showing and telling on the Overhead Projections or finds one example each of showing and telling characterization, preferably relating to one character.
- reads and/or displays these to the class.

TEACHER AND STUDENTS

- complete the sections on the Overhead Projection "To Tell or to Show?" with information from the sample leads about the character's name and his or her traits.
- read the examples of character development from the novels students are reading and identify which character traits are told directly to the reader and which traits the author shows us.

SIGN POST:

More examples books using showing or telling for character development are available in *Becoming Better Writers* by Shelley Peterson, pages 85–86.

Character Development, Telling vs Showing
Excerpt from *Island of the Blue Dolphins**
by Scott O'Dell

Telling

My brother Ramo was only a little boy half my age, which was twelve. He was small for one who had lived so many suns and moons, but quick as a cricket. Also foolish as a cricket when he was excited. For this reason and because I wanted him to help me gather roots and not go running off, I said nothing about the shell I saw or the gull with folded wings.

Showing

Ramo threw out his chest. Around his neck was a string of sea-elephant teeth which someone had left behind. It was much too large for him and the teeth were broken, but they rattled as he thrust the spear down between us.

"You forget that I am the son of Chowig," he said.

* O"Dell, Scott. *Island of the Blue Dolphins*. New York: Dell Publishing, 1960.

Vagabond Readers
©1997 F.P. Hendriks Publishing Ltd.
Permission to reproduce for display

Character Development, Telling vs Showing
Excerpt from *Izzy Willy-Nilly* by Cynthia Voigt

Telling

"A nice girl—that's just exactly what I was. Am.

Most of the people I know don't want to be just nice. They want to be interesting, or exciting, romantic, terrific—something special. I don't think I ever wanted to be more than nice. Nice suited me: pretty but nowhere near beautiful; popular enough, with girls and with boys; although no jock, I could give somebody a respectable game of tennis, and I was one of only three sophomores on the school cheerleading squad. A 'B' student, except for Latin where, for some reason, I got a few A's, I did the work I was told to do and didn't mind school: just a nice person, easy to get along with, fun to have around.

Showing

Rosamunde burst out laughing. "You are so— feminine, do you know that? It's terrific. I'd never think of that—and I'd never dare do it. Unless you come with me, because I'd trust your word about how it looked. Would you do that?" She was tempted.

"I can't go to the mall."

"Why not?"

I didn't answer the truth: Because I don't want to go out and be stared at.

* Voigt, Cynthia. *Izzy Willy-Nilly*. New York: Balantine Books, 1986.

Vagabond Readers
©1997 F.P. Hendriks Publishing Ltd.
Permission to reproduce for display

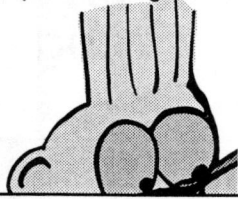

To Tell or To Show?

Book Title: _____

Author: _____

Character's Name: _____

Telling	Showing

Character Development, Part 2

Once students become aware of how published authors develop characters, they may wish to try these techniques in their own writing.

SPECIFIC LEARNER EXPECTATIONS:

• Students are challenged to use the techniques of showing and telling in their own writing.

RESOURCES:

• each student has a book that he or she is reading or has read

• from the previous lesson, Overhead Projection "To Tell or To Show?" on page 118

• age-appropriate Overhead Projection "Character Development, Creating an Opposite" (Excerpts from *I'm Locker 145* for younger readers or from *The Adventures of Tom Sawyer* for older readers)

TEACHER:

• displays the Overhead Projection "Character Development, Creating an Opposite."

• leads a discussion on how the writer revised the character to develop a very different character.

• directs the students to find examples of character development in the stories they are reading (this could be done before the lesson as homework).

• asks students to find a part in the story that gave them a picture of the character in their minds.

• asks students to find parts of the story that made them feel they knew the character or parts where they liked (disliked) the character.

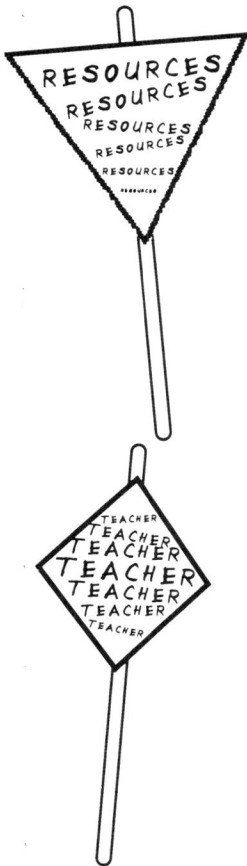

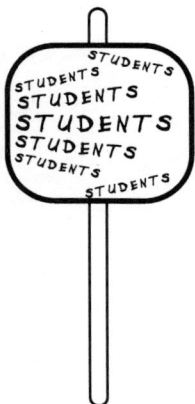

STUDENTS:

- independently or in small groups, complete the Overhead Projection "To Tell or To Show?" for a character in one of their books.

  THEN:

- use these showing and telling character development techniques in a new piece of writing or in an existing piece of writing. Students create their own characters or add to existing characters from stories in their writing folders.

  OR

- using the same technique as their chosen author, create the opposite of the character in their example descriptions

  e.g. change a poor character into a rich one.

TEACHER AND STUDENTS:

- share the characters they create with the class.

Character Development, Creating an Opposite
Original Excerpt from
*I'm Locker 145, Who Are You?** by Sylvia Gunnery

Original

She didn't look out of place sitting in the third row, fifth seat of room 301, class 10M. Her blonde hair hung straight to her shoulders and her pale complexion was marred by only two pimples—probably the result of the chocolate bars she'd been eating as an excuse for something to do other than stand around and stare at everybody before classes started. Her grey sweater did have the blue crest of her old school on it, but it was just a small one. Most of the kids in her class wore jeans and so did she.

Rewrite

She stuck out like a sore thumb sitting in the third row, front seat of room 301, class 10M. Her flaming red hair framed her face in a mass of frizzy curls and her pale complexion was difficult to find under a mass of dark freckles and the acne that her mother kept promising that she'd grow out of. Her gray sweater was emblazoned on the front with the crest of her old school. Most of the kids in her class wore jeans but she had on the short navy blue skirt from her school uniform and those wretched, white knee-high socks that made her knees look more knobby than they truly were. She felt so conspicuous.

* Gunnery, Sylvia. *I'm Locker 145, Who Are You?* Richmond Hill, ON: Scholastic Canada, 1984

Vagabond Readers
© 1997 F.P. Hendriks Publishing Ltd.
Permission to reproduce for display

Character Development, Creating an Opposite
Original Excerpt from
*The Adventures of Tom Sawyer** by Mark Twain

Original
Huckleberry was always dressed in the castoff clothes of full-grown men, and they were in perennial bloom and fluttering with rags. His hat was a vast ruin with a wide crescent lopped out of its brim; his coat, when he wore one, hung nearly to his heels and had the rearward buttons far down the back; but one suspender supported his trousers; the seat of the trousers bagged low and contained nothing; the fringed legs dragged in the dirt when not rolled up.

Rewrite
Bartholomew was always dressed in the finest clothes, made of the finest materials, sewn by the finest tailors in the city. His top hat was made of pure beaver pelt imported from the American colonies. It shimmered with an inner light when the sun hit it. His coat was lamb's wool dyed inky black like his hat. The buttons were of solid brass. His trousers had no creases, proof that they were tailored and not bought off a shelf. He owned trousers in gray and navy blue and for summer wore trousers the color of a fawn. In the front of the trousers there were pleats in which were hidden slash pockets where Bartholomew kept his silver pieces. When he walked one could hear the music these made when jingled together. The legs of the trousers ended in cuffs that brushed the tops of his highly polished leather shoes. Bartholomew was the envy of all the boys raised on Tiller Street down by the docks.

* Twain, Mark. *The Adventures of Tom Sawyer*. New York.

Specific Words and Expressions

SPECIFIC LEARNER EXPECTATIONS

- Students become aware of how the same thing can be said differently and in a more interesting way.
- Students are challenged to find alternatives for overused words in published works and to create a word bank to use in their own writing.

RESOURCES:

- a list of overused or weak words from students' writing
- Overhead Projection "The Dreaded 'Said' and Other Yawners"
- felt pens
- large chart paper
- books that students are reading or have read

TEACHER:

- shows Overhead Projection "The Dreaded Said and Other Yawners."
- uses samples of students' writing or other examples as on page 132 of *Becoming Better Writers** by Shelley Peterson and explains how students can make their own writing more interesting by replacing overused words with more descriptive words.

STUDENTS:

- in small groups receive one to three words from the list of weak words.
- use their books to look for alternative words that authors substitute for these overused words.
- make a list of these alternative words on the chart paper.
- may want to title their charts to indicate the overused word—"Said Replacers."
- can experiment using some of the alternative words in a new or an existing piece of writing.

TEACHER AND STUDENTS:

- do a carousel activity (see page 91) to share the charts with the rest of the class.
- discuss why the alternative words may make the story more interesting.

SIGN POST:

*A related activity can be found in *Becoming Better Writers* by Shelley Peterson published by F.P. Hendriks Publishing, ©1995. "Description: Generating Alternatives for General Words and Expressions" pp. 127–130.

The Dreaded "Said" and Other Yawners

More Yawners:

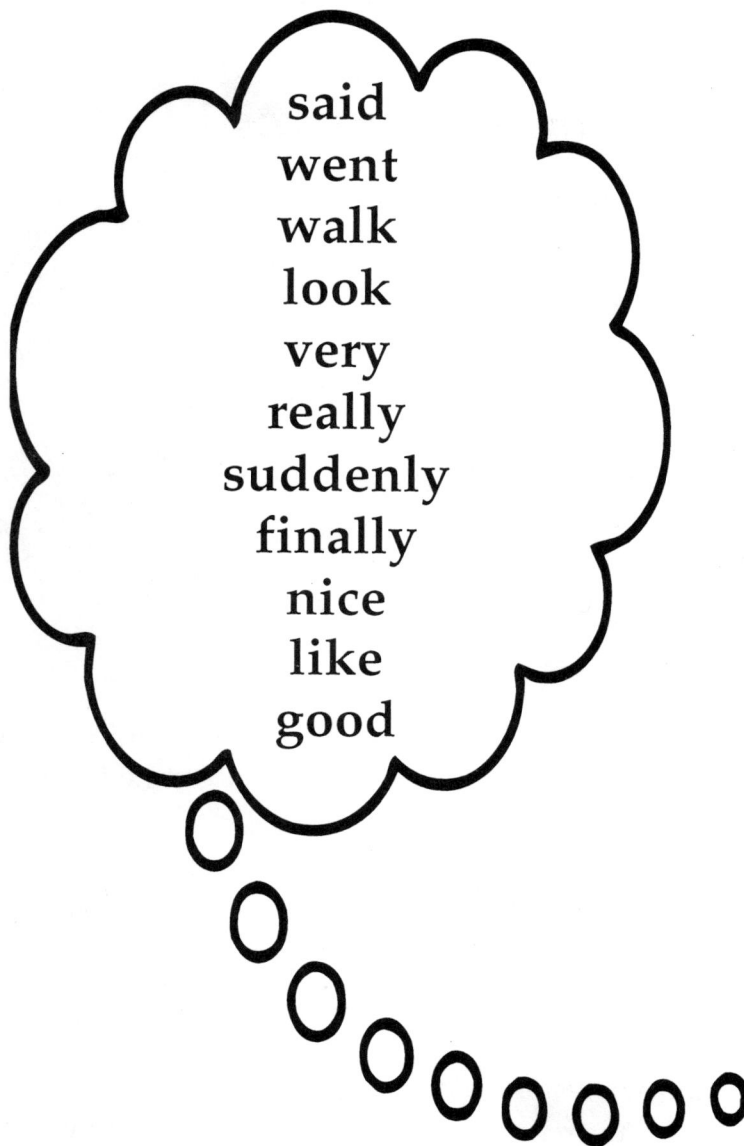

said
went
walk
look
very
really
suddenly
finally
nice
like
good

_____

_____

_____

_____

_____

_____

Point of View

> **SPECIFIC LEARNER EXPECTATIONS:**
> - Students develop an understanding of how point of view affects a story.
> - Students are challenged to experiment with point of view in their own writing.

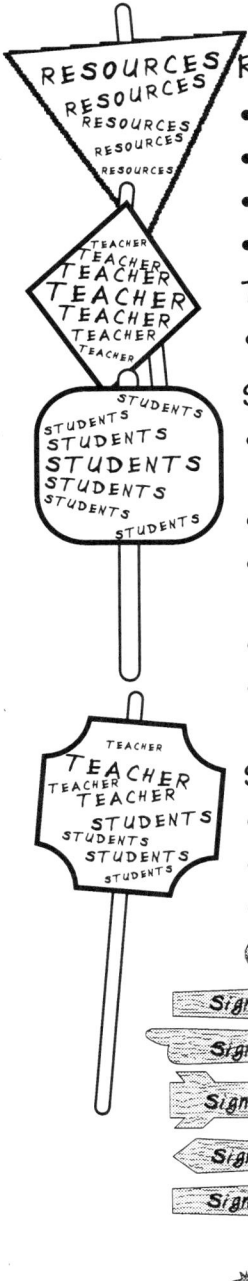

RESOURCES:

- books that the students have previously read
- Overhead Projection "Examples of Point of View"
- Student Performance Master "Identifying Point of View"
- Student Reference "Questions for Evaluating Point of View"

TEACHER:

- shows Overhead Projections "Point of View" or other examples.

STUDENTS:

- choose a situation from a book they have read where the character is in conflict with another character.
- identify who is telling about this situation (narrator or character).
- rewrite the situation from another point of view such as another character or a narrator, depending on how the original situation was written.
- rewrite an existing piece of writing (e.g., a fairy tale) from another point of view.
- evaluate their own writing on their choice of the most effective point of view using the Student Reference "Questions for Evaluating Point of View."

STUDENTS AND TEACHER:

- select passages for students to rewrite.
- share the rewritten situations.
- discuss how the change in point of view could change the story itself.

SIGN POST:

A related activity can be found in *Becoming Better Writers* by Shelley Peterson, published by F.P. Hendriks Publishing, ©1995. "Selecting a Point of View" pages 147–151.

Problems?

Refer to Travel Insurance in Chapter 1 on pages 10–13

Travel Insurance

Examples of Point of View

First Person Point of View:

The dream is too long. It slithers and slips and gurgles deeply into midnight pools in which I see my own face looking back. It pounds with a scream that crashes into earth-torn caverns and is drowned; it surges with the babble of voices that splash against my ears; it whispers over words I can't understand.

From Nixon, Joan Lowery. *The Other Side of Dark*. New York: Dell, Publishing 1986

Third Person Point of View:

And that was the problem with the whole family, B.J. thought gloomily. Entirely too many all-stars. Mom was an all-star, and so was Jodi. She got report cards with comments like, "Jodi is an exceptional student," and "Jodi is a pleasure to have in class." And of course, there was Dad, who was an all-star too—when he was around.

That just left B.J. and Luke. B.J. got report cards with comments like, "Bradley is quite a bright boy, but he doesn't apply himself." And Luke got phone calls from neighbors saying, "If that stupid dog digs up my tulips again, I'll shoot him!"

From Weir, Ian. *The Video Kid*. Richmond Hill, ON: Scholastic, 1988

IDENTIFYING POINT OF VIEW

Title: _____

Author: _____

Point of view used: _____

Excerpt that shows the point of view used:

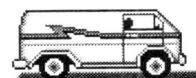

_____

_____

_____

_____

_____

_____

_____

_____

QUESTIONS FOR EVALUATING POINT OF VIEW

Directions: When writing fiction, ask yourself the following questions so that you have a clear idea about how you would like the story to be told.

1. Does the person I have chosen to tell the story know and understand the information I want to communicate to the reader?

   Does it make sense that this character would possess the information?

2. Does the person I have chosen to tell the story give enough information about the characters' actions, thoughts, and feelings?

   Does the person give too much information?

3. Does the person I have chosen to tell the story remain the same all the way through the story?

4. How would the story change if another character told it?

   How would this influence the reader?

   Does this influence have a desirable effect on the story?

Channeling Enthusiasm

Heather: Most of our vagabond readers have read and completed a log entry for at least one novel. They are eager to share their experiences with each other.

Kori: Great! We can let them do that by guiding them through group activities that allow them to explore their novels even further.

Heather: Let's begin by having the students do short biographies on the authors of their novels. Then we can spend more time on characterization. That will give me a chance to teach the students about interviewing techniques.

Kori: Then we can do some work on setting and plot.

Heather: In assessing the log entries, I've noticed that some students have trouble identifying the theme of their novel. Let's incorporate a lesson on theme to help them.

Kori: Great! We can also start planning celebrations to acknowledge the students' reading and writing achievements.

Author Biographies

This activity may be used following the lesson on Folklore and Biographical literature found in Chapter Three, but it also works well at any time throughout the program.

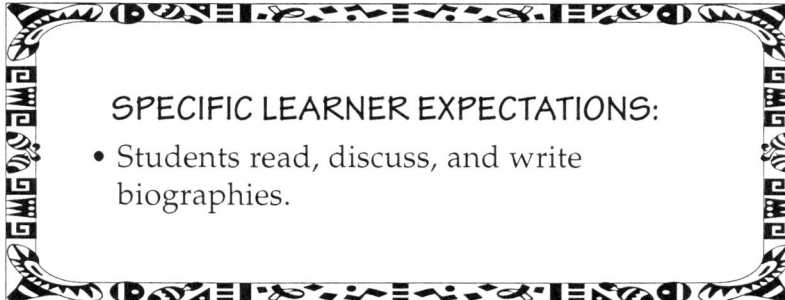

> **SPECIFIC LEARNER EXPECTATIONS:**
> • Students read, discuss, and write biographies.

RESOURCES:

• Overhead Projection "Author Biographies"
• Student Reference "Author Biography: Marilyn Halvorson"
> OR
• an author biography of the teacher's choice

TEACHER:

• reads selected author biography orally to the class.
> OR
• supplies each student with a copy of the selected biography.

TEACHER AND STUDENTS:

• discuss the information included in the biography.
• complete Overhead Projection "Author Biography" for the selected author.

STUDENTS:

• write a biography including the similar information for an author (another student) in the class. Students may choose partners or draw names.
• work in pairs to introduce one another to the class.

SIGN POST:

As you work through this final part of the program, you may wish to continue the travel motif by holding an author's convention at one of the destinations the class will reach or has already reached. All the students are authors attending the convention.

Vagabond Readers

Author Biographies

Name

Personal Facts

Education

Careers
(other than writing)

Motivation to Begin Writing

Author's Work

Awards or Other Recognition

Author Biography

Marilyn Halvorson

Marilyn Halvorson was born in January 1948, in Olds, Alberta. She grew up as an only child on her parents farm/ranch near Sundre, Alberta. Marilyn began writing at the age of twelve when she wrote two pages for a book and then stopped. Later her high school English teacher convinced her to submit a short story she had written to a newspaper. It was rejected but the editor enclosed a positive note. Marilyn says that is when she felt encouraged to be a writer.

After graduation from high school Marilyn began selling stories to CKUA radio and also wrote for her church paper. She received her education degree from the University of Calgary and began teaching junior high school in Sundre where she had attended school. She admits that teaching influences her writing greatly.

In 1982, Marilyn decided to enter the Alberta Writing for Youth Competition. She won the competition with *Cowboys Don't Cry*, which appeared in 1984. Her second novel *Let It Go* followed one year later. *Nobody Said It Would Be Easy* appeared in 1987.

Marilyn still resides on her Sundre ranch with her five horses, a German shepherd, and two cats—one of them three-legged.

Let Me Introduce Myself—Developing Biographies

Like the previous author biography activity, this lesson involves students in investigating human nature. In this case however, students explore the personalities of fictitious people by assuming the roles of characters in their novels.

SPECIFIC LEARNER EXPECTATIONS:

- Students meet characters from novels their classmates are reading.
- Students gain experience in role-playing and interviewing.

RESOURCES:

- student novels
- Student Performance Master "Interview Guidelines"

TEACHER:

- directs students to choose one of the main characters in their novels to role-play.

STUDENTS:

- complete Student Performance Master "Interview Guidelines."
- write a monologue, based on their answers to "Interview Guidelines," showing their character's personality.
- use the monologue to role-play their chosen character for the rest of the class.

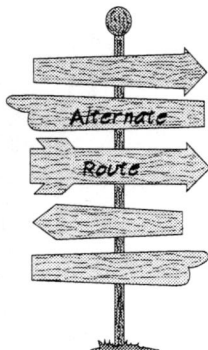

ALTERNATE ROUTE:

Divide students into pairs and have partners interview each other as they are role-playing their fictitious characters using the Student Performance Master "Interview Guidelines" and adding their own questions as needed.

INTERVIEW GUIDELINES

Directions: Imagine you are a character in a novel you have read recently. Answer the questions as you think the character would. If the novel does not supply a particular answer directly, then "invent" an answer based on what you already know about the character.

1. **Name** _____

2. **Background**

    In what town or city do you live?

    Briefly describe your home.

    Tell about your family.

3. **Career and Social Life**

    What do you normally do between nine and four o'clock on weekdays?

    What do you do for recreation?

    Name your friends and briefly describe them.

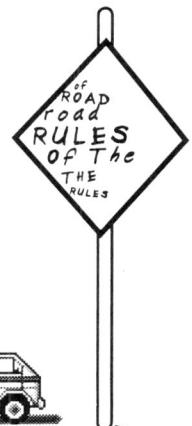

Interview Guidelines, continued

4.   Ambitions

What do you hope to accomplish in the near future?

What issues or problems are important to you?

5.   Personal Characteristics and Role

Describe your personality. Are you friendly? aggressive? reserved?

List the unique qualities or quirks you may have.

How does the central problem of the novel affect you? Are you the antagonist? protagonist?

Sensory Fiesta—Using Your Senses

This extension lesson allows student travelers to use their imaginations to experience scenes and settings their classmates have read about.

> ## SPECIFIC LEARNER EXPECTATIONS:
> - Students gain an appreciation of the way sensory images build atmosphere in fictional settings.
> - Students are exposed to scenes from novels their classmates are reading.

RESOURCES:

- student novels
- six or more scenic pictures from old calendars or magazines

TEACHER:

- supplies examples of sensory images associated with one of the scenic pictures.

   > E.g. A seaside picnic: white color of the sand, pungent smell of the sea, sound of gulls crying, taste of salt, laughter of young people tossing a beach ball around.

- guides students in brainstorming images that appeal to the various senses as the other pictures are viewed.
- divides class into small groups of three to five students.
- gives directions for student activity.

STUDENTS:

- in groups of three to five:
   1. choose a favorite descriptive scene from the novel each group member is reading and make notes about its sensory aspects.
   2. one at a time act as "tour guides," using notes to lead fellow group members, whose eyes may be closed, on an imaginary tour of the scene.
   3. other students may participate orally by comparing their images with those of the tour guide and adjusting them as necessary.
   4. the guide ends the exercise by reading the passage from his or her novel aloud.

Plot Puzzle

As students share the plots of their novels with one another, they also gain a better understanding of the elements of plots and the order in which these elements occur.

SPECIFIC LEARNER EXPECTATIONS:

- Students are introduced to or review the elements of plot.
- Students listen to the plots of novels their classmates are reading.

RESOURCES:

- student novels
- paper
- scissors
- Overhead Projection "Red Riding Hood"

TEACHER:

- presents a series of events that form a familiar plot using Overhead Projection "Red Riding Hood."

TEACHER AND STUDENTS:

- combine the events in a different order.
- decide if the resulting series of events still constitutes a plot. You may wish to do this several times.
- review and/or discuss the requirements of a plot. See the Plot Diagram log entry on page 78.

STUDENTS:

- in pairs:
    1. make a list of the major plot events for a novel each has read.
    2. write or print their lists on a sheet of paper, leaving space between the events so that they can be cut apart.
    3. cut the events apart and mix them up.
    4. trade the strips and figure out the order in which the events occurred in their partner's book.
    5. discuss completed puzzles with their partner to see if they identified the actual plot.

Red Riding Hood

Red Riding Hood prepares a basket of goodies for Grandmother.

Red Riding Hood walks through the woods.

Wolf sees Red Riding Hood.

Wolf takes Grandmother's place in her bed.

Red Riding Hood is surprised by Grandmother's appearance.

Wolf tries to eat Red Riding Hood.

Woodcutter kills Wolf.

Red Riding Hood goes home.

Themes 'n' Schemes—Identifying Themes

This lesson includes a student performance master that helps students to identify, through a short series of steps, the main ideas or themes of their novels.

SPECIFIC LEARNER EXPECTATIONS:

- Students identify novel themes.
- Students hear about themes from novels their classmates are reading.

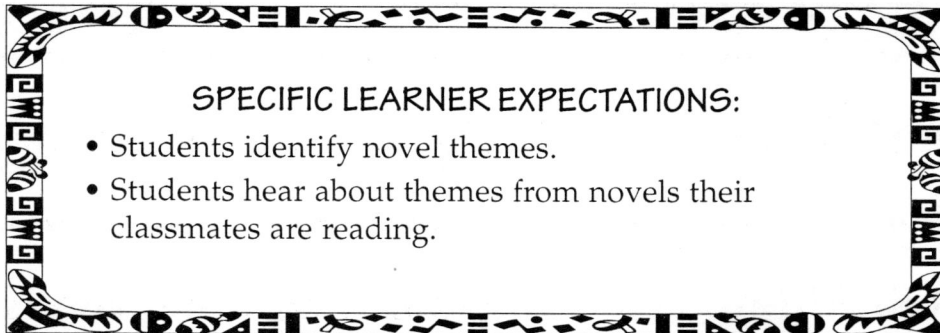

RESOURCES:

- student novels
- Student Performance Master "Plucking Pearls"

TEACHER:

- leads a brief discussion on what is meant by a story's theme.
- gives examples of common themes:

    e.g. "Determination triumphs over adversity."

    "To master our fears, we must face them."

    "Love conquers all."

STUDENTS:

- individually or in pairs, complete Student Performance Master "Plucking Pearls." If students are allowed to discuss possible themes in pairs, they may be better able to extract the theme and develop a single statement to describe it.
- discuss and/or debate the themes expressed by students in their final oyster shell statements.

STUDENT PERFORMANCE MASTER

NAME _____

PLUCKING PEARLS

Directions: Complete the blanks with information from your novel. The activity should lead you to the "pearl of wisdom" the author is attempting to give you through his or her novel. Think of a statement that summarizes what the novel says about life and write it on the lines in the oyster shell.

This book is about a character named _____

who is affected by a conflict involving _____

In trying to reach his or her goal of _____

he or she is aided by _____

_____

and hindered by _____

_____

The character finally achieves _____

and comes to realize that _____

Write the theme of your novel here. ✐➔

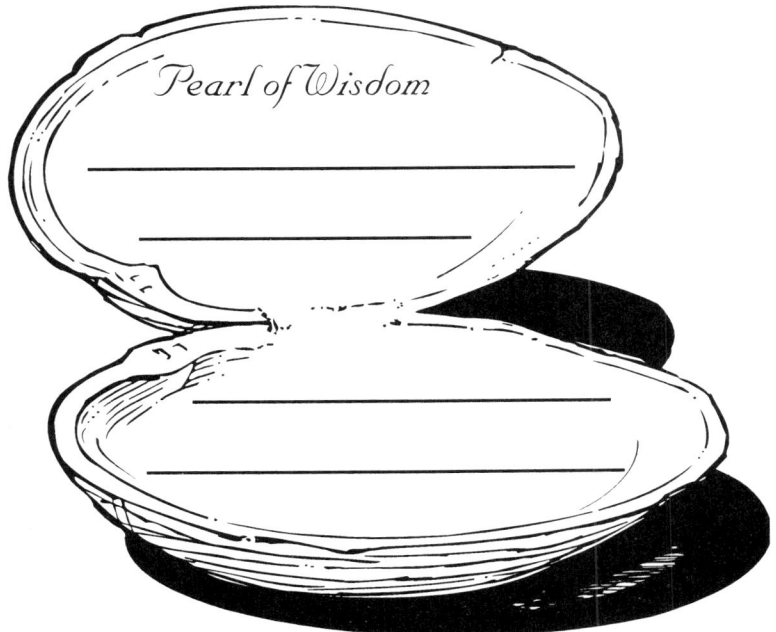

Pearl of Wisdom

Celebrating the Novel

At some point during the program and then towards the end of the school year you may wish to have the students celebrate their success in reaching their destinations by sharing, more formally, one or more of the novels they have read.

SPECIFIC STUDENT EXPECTATIONS:

• Students create, perform, write and/or do research on some aspect of one or more novels they have been reading.

RESOURCES:

• Student Reference "Celebrating Throughout the Year"
• Student Reference "Celebrating at Year's End"
• Student Performance Master "Planning My Novel Celebration"

TEACHER:

• reviews the activities on either Student Reference from which students can choose to celebrate their reading successes.
• reviews expectations for quality and quantity of work depending on students' abilities and time available.
• sets a schedule for the celebrations.
• reviews students' plans to ensure an acceptable standard of performance.

STUDENTS:

• choose one or more activities to complete on some aspect of their novels.
• completes Student Performance Master "Planning My Novel Celebration" to assist in planning how they will carry out the activity chosen.

SIGN POST:

You may wish to use these activities as the main events or sessions during an author convention or you may hold a travel fair where students set up booths to display their work.

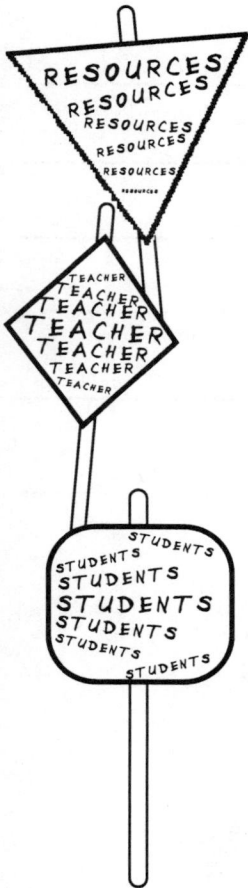

CELEBRATING THROUGHOUT THE YEAR

Art or Design

1. Have a fashion show of clothing that may have been worn by one or two of the story's characters or that reflect its setting.

2. Draw, sculpt, or paint your favorite character.

3. Draw or paint a scene from the book, or make a cartoon drawing illustrating a short section of the plot (action sequence).

4. Design a book jacket for your novel including cover art, plot summary, endorsements, a list of other books by the same author, and an author biography.

5. Make a diorama, game, or video based on the novel.

Writing or Composition

1. Rewrite the ending of a story, or begin the sequel to a story that ended "too soon." Go further into the lives of the characters.

2. Interview someone in the community who has the same occupation as your favorite character. Share your findings with the class.

3. Make up a scrapbook of newspaper or magazine articles related to a book or series of books, e.g. sports stories.

4. Compose an original song based on the story, or write a short play involving two or more of its characters.

Drama or Performance Art

1. Perform a selection of music that might be included in a movie based on the novel, or construct a movie poster advertising it.

2. Give an oral summary of your book and then allow other students in the class to ask questions. This could also be done in panel format if more than one student has read your book.

3. Stage a radio or TV interview with an antagonist from the novel to discover his or her side of the story.

CELEBRATING AT YEAR'S END

Research

1. Research a social issue that may have been included in the theme of a book, e.g. drug or alcohol abuse, divorce, child abuse, animal abuse or neglect. Develop an interesting way to share the information you have discovered.

2. Research the historical event of a story, e.g. World War II as it relates to *The Diary of Anne Frank*. Design a visual method of sharing the information and how it relates to the novel.

3. Research the technology that may make a science fiction story possible in years to come, e.g. life on other planets, colonizing the moon. Try to use visuals and some of the technology used in your novel.

4. Research the training or schooling required in order to do what one of your favorite characters does in a story, e.g. doctor, mountain climber. Make a wall-sized chart of the information including visuals.

5. Research the life of your favorite author. Construct a time line that shows this information.

6. Research the process that is followed in order to make movies from written stories. Try making a movie of one of your own stories and have a screening for your class.

7. Research how a book is published and marketed. Publish a book of your own writing.

8. Research how books were printed and published in the days before printing presses. Share the methods in an interesting way.

9. Research how books were printed and published in the days before computers. Share the methods in an interesting way.

10. Research the culture of a people whose myths and folklore you have read. Design and construct a diorama showing some aspects of this culture.

11. Survey the students in your school and find out which type of fiction is most frequently read. Design a questionnaire and a method to display your results, e.g. wall-size graph, chart.

12. Prepare foods that may have been eaten in your novel. Have a class "food fair" or a "tasting" sharing these dishes with the class.

STUDENT PERFORMANCE MASTER

PLANNING MY NOVEL CELEBRATION

NAME _____

Name _____ Grade _____ Class _____

Activity Title _____

ACTIVITY DESCRIPTION. In four or five sentences describe what you will do to celebrate your novel.

_____

_____

_____

_____

_____

RELATIONSHIP TO NOVEL. Explain how the activity you have chosen is related to the novel.

_____

_____

_____

MATERIALS. List here all the materials you will need to complete your activity.

_____

_____

_____

_____

SOURCES. List here all of the places you will get the materials you need.

_____

_____

_____

AUDIENCE AND PRESENTATION. Describe how you will present your activity and explain who your audience will be.

_____

_____

_____

NOTES

For Your Information

Heather and I have gathered various tools for traveling that we have developed for both teacher and student use. We have included both assessment and record-keeping tools. We hope these will be useful in the implementation of the **Vagabond Readers** program.

Tools for Traveling

Assessment Tools

The Assessment Masters in this Appendix may be used as they are or adapted to suit your needs. Included are

- Assessment Checklist for Log Entries
- Answer Sheet for Overhead Projection "Mechanical Matters Part 1"
- Answer Sheet for Overhead Projection "Mechanical Matters Part 2"
- Answer Sheet for Student Performance Master "Graphing a Path"

Record-keeping for the Teacher

The record-keeping forms in this section may be used as they are or adapted to suit your needs. Included are

- Record of Completed Student Performance Masters
- Record of Participation in Sharing Activities
- Record of Reading Log Entries
- Record of Celebration Projects

Record-keeping for Students

The record-keeping forms in this section may be used as they are or adapted to suit the students' needs. Included are

- "Tracks Record" for recording the books a student reads on his or her journey
- "Travel Schedule" to help students plan a schedule for their reading

ASSESSMENT CHECKLIST FOR LOG ENTRIES

Student Name: _____

Book Title: _____

Book Author: _____

Log Entry #

_____

Requirements	Acceptable? ✔/✗	Possible Grade	Actual Grade
Summary Paragraph or Notes		14	
Bibliography		2	
Classification		2	
Presentation		2	
TOTAL		20	

ASSESSMENT CHECKLIST FOR LOG ENTRIES

Student Name: _____

Book Title: _____

Book Author: _____

Log Entry #

_____

Requirements	Acceptable? ✔/✗	Possible Grade	Actual Grade
Summary Paragraph or Notes		14	
Bibliography		2	
Classification		2	
Presentation		2	
TOTAL		20	

Mechanical Matters, Part 1 (page 62)

Choyce, Lesley. <u>Good Idea Gone Bad</u>.* Halifax, NS: Formac, 1993.

Mackay, Claire. <u>The Minerva Program</u>.* Toronto, ON: James Lorimer, 1984.

Rinaldi, Ann. <u>The Last Silk Dress</u>.* New York: Bantam, 1988.

Wells, Rosemary. <u>When No One Was Looking</u>.* New York: Scholastic, 1980.

Use the bibliography above to answer the following:

1. The publisher of *The Last Silk Dress* is ___*Bantam*___.

2. The author of *The Minerva Program* is___*Claire Mackay*___.

3. Scholastic published a book by Rosemary Wells in the year___*1980*___.

4. The book by Lesley Choyce was published in the city of___*Halifax*___.

*Book titles are generally identified by using italics and where italics are not possible, by underlining.

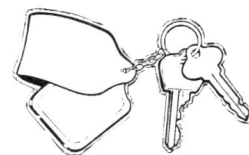

Mechanical Matters, Part 2 (page 63)

Insert punctuation as required:

1. Christopher, Matt. <u>Wingman on Ice</u>.* Boston, MA: Little, Brown & Co., 1964.

2. Bennett, Jay. <u>The Skeleton Man</u>.* New York: Ballantine, 1986.

3. Jacobs, Paul Samuel. <u>Born into Light</u>.* New York: Scholastic, 1988.

Insert punctuation, underline and capitalize as required:

4. Hunt, Irene. <u>Up a Road Slowly</u>.* New York: Berkley, 1966.

5. Beagle, Peter S. <u>The Last Unicorn</u>.* New York: Ballantine, 1968.

6. Frank B. Gilbreth, Jr. and Ernestine Gilbreth Carey are a brother and sister who co-authored a book entitled *Cheaper by the Dozen.* It was copyrighted in 1948 and published in Toronto by Bantam Books. Make a bibliographic entry for this book.

Carey, Ernestine Gilbreth, and Frank B. Gilbreth Jr. <u>Cheaper by the Dozen</u> . Toronto: Bantam, 1948.

*Book titles are generally identified by using italics and where italics are not possible, by underlining.

GRAPHING A PATH (Page 64)

Directions: Use the following bibliography to answer the questions below.

Bibliography

Hughes, Monica. *My Name is Paula Popowich!* Toronto, ON: James Lorimer, 1983.

Naylor, Phyllis Reynolds. *The Keeper*. Toronto, ON: Bantam, 1986.

Peck, Richard. *Remembering the Good Times*. New York: Dell, 1985.

Snyder, Carol. *The Leftover Kid*. New York: Berkley, 1986.

---

1. The publisher of *Remembering the Good Times* is _____**Dell**_____.

2. Naylor's book was published in the city of _____**Toronto**_____ by _____**Bantam**_____.

3. The author of *The Leftover Kid* is _____**Carol Snyder**_____.

4. The book by Monica Hughes was published in the year _____**1983**_____.

5. Insert the correct punctuation for the following two books:

> Callahan, Steven. <u>Adrift</u>. New York: Ballantine, 1986.

> Nelson, O.T. <u>The Girl Who Owned a City</u>. New York: Dell, 1975.

6. Rewrite the following bibliographic entry. Insert punctuation, underline, and capitalize as required.

Paulsen, Gary. <u>The Crossing</u>. New York: Orchard, 1987.

8. Write a bibliographic entry for Victoria M. Althoff's book entitled *Key to My Heart*, published in 1989 by Willowisp Press of Worthington, Ohio.

Althoff, Victoria M. <u>Key to My Heart</u>. Worthington, OH: Willowisp, 1989.

*Book titles are generally identified by using italics and where italics are not possible, by underlining.

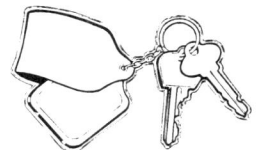

Record-keeping for Teachers

What follows are some suggestions that may help you to simplify and to streamline your record-keeping and assessment procedures.

- To simplify marking you may prefer not to assign grades for log entries submitted, but rather give the student a checkmark, sticker, or stamp for an acceptably completed product that includes the required documentation and information about the novel. You may then require that any omissions or errors of presentation (e.g., spelling, sentence construction, and so on) be corrected before the sticker or stamp is awarded. In this case you may wish to incorporate the students' contracted marks into only the final report.

- Celebration and related writing projects can be evaluated like any other language arts assignments, with grades incorporated directly into the students' overall language arts performance assessment.

- You may prefer to simply record student participation in the oral sharing activities rather than assign marks. The primary purpose of these activities is to build the interest of students in books their classmates are reading and to provide opportunities for informal, enjoyable discussion.

- You may prefer to give the primary responsibility of record-keeping to the students. The following page provides suggestions for organizing student record-keeping.

Record-keeping for Students

A set of records should be made available to students so that they can monitor their own progress.

- Student-accessible records may take the form of attractive wall posters, created and decorated by the students. Reading achievements may be tracked using stickers, stamps, initials, or checkmarks placed on the charts by the individual students. Younger students may be motivated to read by collecting stickers of dinosaurs or other pictures from a favorite topic of study. If charts are publicly displayed, we suggest dividing the class into groups and tracking the progress of teams, rather than individuals, on these records. Students may enjoy choosing a name for their team and may even find or design stickers to fit the name.

- Students may assist in creating a map on which a highway or flight route is marked, along with various destinations corresponding to student goals (see "Sack of Suggestions," page 14). The students can place drawings or cutouts of various modes of transportation on the classroom map to keep track of the number of books they have read. The markers are placed at the appropriate milestones as the teams or individuals progress toward their reading goals. If their personal reading achievements are being displayed on public records, students may wish to use code names known only to the teacher. Stickers or stamps may even be designed to match the code name.

- If a simpler method of record-keeping is preferred, a wall chart listing student names or teams will suffice. An enlarged, mounted version of the "Record of Log Entries" on page 158 may be used for this purpose. Students may then use rubber stamps, stickers, or felt pens to do their own record-keeping, choosing a stamp, sticker, or their initials to mark the successful completion of each book and log entry. Again, students may prefer to use code names on these charts. Some basic record-keeping forms are provided on pages 156–161 to help you get started, but you are encouraged to tailor this program to complement other topics you may be studying in your classroom.

- Students in higher grades (e.g., eight and nine) will likely wish to keep their own individual records. Student record-keeping may be done on sheets of graph paper or on the form supplied on page 160 inserted in the students' Language Arts notebooks or on special cards kept in their log books.

- The "Travel Schedule" on page 161 is intended to help students organize and "stick to" a reading schedule to ensure they reach their reading destinations. Not all students will need such a schedule, but it may help parents who may have difficulty encouraging their children to read. Students can complete the calendar with all the activities they are involved in so that they can plan their reading times more effectively.

Appendix: Keeping Track

RECORD-KEEPING CLASS _____

RECORD OF COMPLETED STUDENT PERFORMANCE MASTERS

Dates or Titles →

Students' Names ▼

Vagabond Readers
©1997 F.P. Hendriks Publishing Ltd.
Permission to reproduce

Appendix: Keeping Track

CLASS _____

RECORD OF PARTICIPATION IN SHARING ACTIVITIES

Dates or Titles→

Students' Names ▶

Vagabond Readers

Appendix: Keeping Track

RECORD-KEEPING

CLASS _____

RECORD OF COMPLETED LOG ENTRIES

Students' Names ▶	Dates →	October	November	December	January	February	March	April	May	June

Appendix: Keeping Track

CLASS _____

RECORD OF CELEBRATION PROJECTS

Students' Names ▶

Dates or Titles →

Vagabond Readers
© 1997 F.P. Hendriks Publishing Ltd.

STUDENT RECORD-KEEPING

Appendix: Keeping Track

"TRACKS" RECORD

NAME _____

Books Read ▼	Dates →	October	November	December	January	February	March	April	May	June

Vagabond Readers

Appendix: Keeping Track

TRAVEL SCHEDULE

SUNDAY	MONDAY	TUESDAY	WEDNESDAY	THURSDAY	FRIDAY	SATURDAY

For the Month of _____

NOTES

Glossary of Library and Literary Terms

Vagabond Readers
©1997 F.P. Hendriks Publishing Ltd.

For Your Information

In this book, Kori and I have used many terms specific to literature and libraries. To help everyone, teachers and students alike remain consistent in their understanding and use of the terms, we have provided a glossary. This may be used as a teacher reference or may be photocopied and distributed to students.

These definitions are provided as a guide. Individual teachers may wish to adapt definitions to suit their programs.

GLOSSARY OF LIBRARY AND LITERARY TERMS

Added Entry	an additional catalog entry for a particular item, other than the main entry
Antagonist	a character or force that opposes or acts against the main character in a story
Author	the person responsible for the intellectual or artistic content of a work
Autobiography	a literary work in which the author tells the story of his or her own life
Bibliography	an alphabetized list of books or resources, with one entry per item, on a particular subject or by a specific person or group of people
Biography	a literary work telling the story of a real person's life
Body	the part of a catalog entry that begins with the title and ends with information about the item's publication; also the main part of an essay or research paper
Book	a collection of more than 48 bound pages bearing a distinctive title
Call Number	the symbolic notation used to identify a particular work and to indicate its placement in the library
Card Catalog	a library catalog consisting of 7.5 cm x 12.5 cm (3 inch x 5 inch) cards
Catalog	a list of the materials held in a particular library
Character	one of the fictional people in a story
Circulation Desk	the area in the library where outgoing and incoming materials are processed
Climax	the turning point or "high" point of a story, where the action is most intense

Complication	an event that represents a clash of ideas, interests or opinions and gets the reader more involved in the story; occurs after the initiating incident; a novel contains many complications
Computer Catalog	a library catalog accessed through a computer program
Conflict	a problem or struggle faced by the main character in a story
Copyright	the legal right to publish, reprint, and sell a literary or artistic work for a specific number of years
Denouement	from the French meaning "unknotting"; follows the final outcome of a story; often deals with the future of the characters
Dewey Decimal	a number corresponding to a particular subject; from a library classification system developed by Melvil Dewey in 1876
Exposition	presentation of background or explanatory information needed to understand the story; includes information on setting, characters, and social circumstance
Fable	a brief tale or story that has a moral or teaches a useful lesson, often using animal characters that speak and act like human beings
Falling Action	the events that follow a story's climax and lead to the plot's resolution
Fantasy	a fictional story giving little or no useful information about a cultural group, that relates an ordinary person's struggle to deal with a supernatural or magical situation or a hero's quest to achieve a goal by overcoming negative or evil forces
Fiction	a written work that is the product of a writer's imagination and may or may not be based on fact
Flashback	a writing technique in which the author refers to past events in order to provide essential information

Folklore a general term given to tales, songs, sayings, and dances that are passed down from generation to generation in certain social or cultural groups, and that convey the beliefs, customs, traditions, or values of the people in those groups

Folktale a traditional story that is also anonymous, timeless, and placeless, handed down (often orally) by the common people of a country or region from one generation to the next

Foreshadowing a technique authors use to provide hints or clues about what is going to happen in the novel

Genre a distinct class or category of literary work characterized by a particular form

Historical Fiction a story that realistically shows how people lived during a particular period in history

Initiating Incident the event in a story that introduces the conflict

International Standard Book Number (ISBN) an internationally agreed upon number that identifies a particular item

Legend a popular story handed down from earlier times; often seen as historical although it cannot be verified

Literature written works dealing with ideas of universal or timeless interest and characterized by excellence of form or expression

Main Entry a full catalog entry bearing the author's name and all other information necessary for the identification of a work, that serves as the basis for all other entries that describe a particular item

Modern Realistic a fictional story that is realistic and has a modern setting

Myth a traditional story that uses supernatural beings and events to explain a cultural belief, a practice, or a natural phenomenon

Nonfiction	a written work that gives factual information about a subject or topic
Novel	a fictional work of considerable length having a plot that is revealed by the actions, speech, and thoughts of its characters
Pamphlet	a printed, paper-covered publication of forty-nine pages or fewer
Periodical	a publication issued at regular intervals in successive parts, each with the same title but a different volume number
Place of Publication	the city in which a literary work is produced
Plot	the pattern of events in a story, built around a series of events that involve the characters
Point of View	the perspective from which a story is told
Protagonist	the main or leading character in a story
Publisher	the individual or corporate body responsible for issuing a work
Pulp Fiction	a story of questionable literary merit that nevertheless may have a high degree of emotional appeal for its intended audience
Resolution	the final outcome of a story's problem or conflict; how the problem in the story is dealt with
Rising Action	the events in a story that lead to the climax
Science Fiction	a story that deals with actual or imagined knowledge and its impact on individuals or society
Series	a number of separate works usually related to one another in subject matter or form, often issued in succession by the same publisher, and having individual titles as well as a common title known as the series title

Setting	the time, place, and social circumstances in which a story occurs
Theme	the meaning or main point of the story that often helps readers understand themselves and others
Title	the name given to a particular work
Vertical File	a collection of unbound materials such as pamphlets, clippings, or illustrations, usually kept in folders in a filing cabinet

NOTES

Language Arts Titles from F.P. Hendriks Publishing

Book 1

Becoming Better Writers
by Shelley Peterson
• contains practical information to help teachers pass on successful fiction-writing techniques to students
• includes sample lessons, overheads, wall chart ideas, annotated bibliographies, and assessment checklists
• intended for grades 3–9
• coil bound, 8.5 x 11 format, 176 pages

E. Dunn of Massachusetts says "*Becoming Better Writers* is great!"

Book 2

Teaching Conventions Unconventionally
by Shelley Peterson
• the second book in the *Becoming Better Writers Series* for grades 3–9
• the ultimate companion for teachers who are frustrated by the need to teach writing conventions but who wish to avoid dull, unproductive worksheets
• includes mini-lessons, student performance masters, overhead projections, teacher references, student references, samples of student writing, hand-outs for parents
• coil bound, 8.5 x 11 format, 264 pages

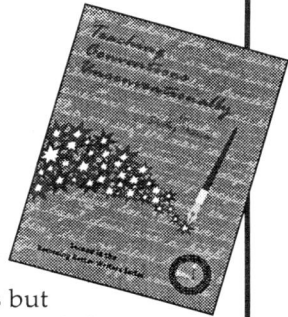

AN IMPORTANT ANNOUNCEMENT

We are pleased to announce that **Becoming Better Writers** has just been named as a designated resource for the Western Canada Protocol for English/Language Arts.

Bring the classroom into the library and the library into the classroom.

Vagabond Readers by H. Jarmin & F. Korithoski
• complements the reading aspect of the *Becoming Better Writers* series and helps students make the reading-writing connection
• encourages independent reading and helps students to use the library for discovery learning.
• contains lessons, strategies for getting students to read a variety of genres, overhead projections, student performance masters, wall chart samples, and organizational charts
• intended for grades 4–9
• coil bound, 8.5 x 11 format, 170 pages

Coming Spring 1998!

From Your Child's Teacher, by Dr. R. Bright, L. McMullin & D. Platt
• is for parents who wish to help their children be effective communicators
• helps parents understand various teaching methods
• demonstrates how parents can supplement literacy lessons taught in the classroom
• can be used by teachers to show parents how children learn
• includes hand-outs for parents
• coil bound, 5.5 X 8.5 inch format, 154 pages

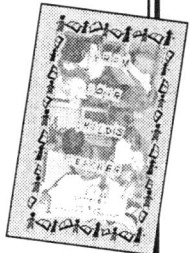

Please send the following:

Product Name		Quantity	Cost
Becoming Better Writers, ISBN 0-9699619-0-1	$23.95 (CDN) $16.95 (US)	X ____	= _____
Vagabond Readers ISBN 0-9699619-3-6	$24.95 (CDN) $17.95 (US)	X ____	= _____
Teaching Conventions Unconventionally ISBN 0-9682970-2-1	$27.95 (CDN) $19.95 (US)	X ____	= _____
From Your Child's Teacher ISBN 0-9682970-3-X	$19.95 (CDN) $14.95 (US)	X ____	= _____

Shipping and handling ($3.50 minimum for a maximum of two products)   _____

Ontario, Quebec & Maritimes customers add $1.00 to S&H   _____

US customers add $2.00 to S&H   _____

Subtotal   _____

Tax (Canadian customers add G.S.T (.07 X subtotal)   _____

Total   _____

Check method of payment: ❐ Check ❐ Purchase Order #_____ (Please include) ❐ VISA (only)

Name _____

School _____

Address _____

City _____ Province _____

Postal Code _____

Phone _____ Fax _____

Visa# _____ Expiry Date _____

Signature _____

VISA

HENDRIKS PUBLISHING LTD.

Canada
4806–53 St.
Stettler, AB, Canada
T0C 2L2

USA
1214 Flint Hill Road
Wilmington, DE, USA
19808-1914

Phone/Fax: (403)-742-6483
Toll Free Phone/Fax: 1-888-374-8787
E-mail: hendriks@telusplanet.net
Website: www.telusplanet.net/public/hendriks

Workshops for Teachers of Language Arts
Given by Authors Who Are Experienced Teachers

The Vagabond Readers Workshop

Given by teacher Heather Jarmin and librarian Francis Korithoski, this workshop shows how to bring the classroom to the library and the library to the classroom. It outlines how to easily implement a well-organized program for promoting independent reading, making efficient use of the library, and making the reading-writing connection so vital to literacy learning.

Workshops by Shelley Peterson

Becoming Better Writers

This workshop introduces mini-lesson ideas and performance based assessment tools to use as starting points for helping students to draw on personal experiences, published literature, and popular films to craft rich, vibrant stories. Strategies for encouraging reluctant writers to write, revise, and edit stories are included.

Classroom Possibilities: Encouraging Students' Revisions of Their Writing

Like the Polaroid picture that becomes increasingly clearer over time, writing is a constant process of revision and of bringing ideas into sharper focus. This session presents informal and formal learning activities that encourage students to view revision as more than a final stage in their writing processes.

From Tiger to Anansi: Encouraging Students to Write <u>Their</u> Stories

In a climate of accountability, there is a danger that students will write for the sake of the test or the grade and as a result students' voices will be lost. Drawing on Anansi the spider's wisdom, this session addresses ways in which students can experience success as writers whose voices are honored regardless of the climate.

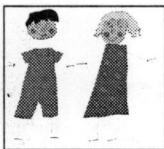

From Your Child's Teacher

Given by a one or more of the authors who are teachers as well as parents, this workshop can be targeted for teachers or parents. It gives teachers strategies for communicating what is happening in the classroom with parents. It can help parents understand the methodologies teachers use in the classroom and give them strategies for fostering literacy at home.

For more information, contact
F.P. Hendriks Publishing

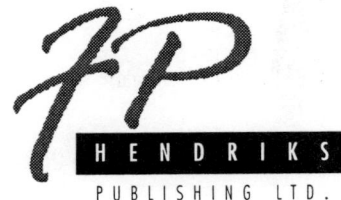

FP HENDRIKS PUBLISHING LTD.

Canada
4806–53 St.
Stettler, AB, Canada
T0C 2L2

USA
1214 Flint Hill Road
Wilmington, DE, USA
19808-1914

Phone/Fax: (403)-742-6483
Toll Free Phone/Fax: 1-888-374-8787
E-mail: hendriks@telusplanet.net